MW01601288

I love Islam,

But

I'm Tired of Muslims

How Spiritual Abuse and Racial Trauma Intersect to Cause Psychological Distress Among African American Muslims

By

Dr. Yusuf Malik Frederick, JD. PhD.

Dedication

This book is dedicated to my parents, Rufus and Dulcia, both of whom would be proud of this work had they been alive to see it, and my grandchildren yet to be born.

Table of Contents

Acknowledgements

I am deeply grateful to my doctoral Chair, whose confidence in me and in this emerging area of psychology never wavered. Thank you for believing in my potential and for supporting a topic that sits at the margins of mainstream discourse. You helped turn uncertainty into possibility and made this work possible.

My sincere thanks to Dr. Verace, my subject-matter expert, for offering some of the most critical, insightful, and generous commentary I have ever received. Your careful reviews, thoughtful challenges, and unwavering commitment to excellence strengthened this dissertation in countless ways.

To my children: you are my daily inspiration. Your curiosity, resilience, and love drive me to be my best self and to leave a legacy of compassion, integrity, and courage for you to follow. Everything I do is for you.

Most of all, I am profoundly thankful for my loving and supportive wife, Renee. You have stood by my side every minute of every day, through the late nights, the doubt, and the hard work. Your patience, encouragement, and faith in me have sustained me beyond measure. Your support is more than words can capture; this dissertation is as much yours as it is mine. Thank you for being my rock, my partner, and my truest champion.

Preface

Despite growing evidence that spiritual abuse and racial trauma independently contribute to psychological distress, their intersection within racially marginalized faith communities remains poorly understood. African American Muslims are notably underrepresented in research on religious harm and race-based stress, leaving a critical gap in knowledge about how congregational power dynamics and anti-Blackness jointly produce psychospiritual injury. This book addresses that gap by examining the combined effects of spiritually abusive experiences and race-based stress on mental health and by exploring institutional mechanisms that translate congregational practices into individual harm. The study is grounded in an intersectionality-informed minority-stress framework and draws on concepts of institutional betrayal and moral-epistemic injury to orient inquiry into multi-level sources of harm.

This research combined surveys and in-depth interviews. Participants were African American Muslim adults with experience in Muslim congregations, recruited through community networks and online. Surveys measured spiritual abuse, racial trauma, depression, anxiety, and feeling morally or intellectually harmed. The data was analyzed both separately and together, and compared with the interview findings. The interviews asked open-ended questions to learn people's stories and find common themes about leadership, religious practices, and how survivors cope (see Appendix A). The study looked for patterns and unique differences to better understand how these harms happen.

The study results indicate that spiritual abuse and racial trauma frequently co-occur and operate synergistically, making psychological distress worse. The quantitative findings documented robust associations among the variables, indicating strong links among these experiences that lead to ongoing distress. Thematic analysis identified three institutional mechanisms, epistemic marginalization, doctrinal weaponization, and institutional betrayal, through which congregational norms and leadership practices undermined spiritual agency, eroded testimonial credibility, and damaged communal trust.

These examples help clarify the broader ideas explored in the study. Overall, these results reconceptualize spiritual abuse among racially marginalized religious contexts as an intersectional public-health issue and call for culturally and spiritually informed clinical care, congregational accountability, survivor-centered policy, and future community-engagement. This research calls for mental health care, survivor-focused policies, and more community-based research to improve support and to reform institutions.

Part I

Framing the Problem

Chapter 1:

Love of Faith, Pain from Community

"I was mentally finished with life. I went into the room, and I put the letter out for my daughters, and I took more pills..." (Bala, 2026). This account came from one of five anonymized interviews for my dissertation research. The interview explored the impact of spiritual abuse on a woman who had suffered harsh treatment from her intensely religious husband. Religion can heal, but it can also harm. This book grows out of my research about compound trauma involving spiritual abuse, and the painful contradictions I encountered in my private life and in my ministry.

For many people, faith brings meaning, courage, and community. Yet the same communities that sustain faith can also cause spiritual injury and deep psychological distress. More than thirty years after my conversion to Islam and drawing on my earlier work as a Christian minister, I saw this pattern repeated across religious traditions. The teachings may be perfect, but practices and human institutions are not. This book examines that tension, its causes and consequences, and what communities might do to prevent spiritual harm.

In my doctoral dissertation that precedes this book, I examined how spiritually abusive dynamics within Muslim congregational contexts intersect with race-based traumatic stress to produce compounded psychological harm. The present book builds on that work to make the phenomenon accessible to clinicians, religious leaders, survivors, and scholars while centering the lived experiences of African American Muslims who have navigated both religious devotion and betrayal. This first chapter introduces the research problem, purpose, and significance. It explains why African American Muslims are a critical focus, defines the core constructs used throughout the text, summarizes the mixed-methods study that informs the narrative, and offers a roadmap for readers.

Introduction

Spiritual abuse (SA) is increasingly recognized as a multifaceted and underacknowledged form of psychological and emotional harm, wherein religious beliefs, spiritual teachings, or sacred authority are weaponized to manipulate, exploit, or exert control over individuals or groups (Awaad & Riaz, 2022; Oakley et al., 2024). While often obscured by the trusted and sacred contexts in which it occurs, SA can leave lasting psychological and emotional wounds, damaging an individual's sense of self, spiritual autonomy, and mental well-being. It typically manifests through coercive practices such as doctrinal distortion, spiritual gaslighting, and the misuse of religious authority to instill guilt, fear, and compliance.

This form of harm does not occur in isolation. Instead, it often exists within broader systems of oppression, particularly in marginalized communities where faith and identity are deeply intertwined. Within the African American Muslim community, an understudied and growing segment of the U.S. Muslim population, spiritual abuse frequently intersects with the cumulative effects of racial trauma. Members of this community navigate a unique socio-religious space shaped by both intra-religious hierarchies and the enduring legacies of systemic racism. These overlapping forms of harm compound the psychological toll of spiritual abuse, deepening feelings of alienation and distress (Ellis et al., 2023; Panchuk, 2020).

The African American Muslim community represents a significant and growing segment of the U.S. Muslim population. According to the Pew Research Center, Black Muslims account for approximately 20% of all U.S. Muslims, with about half being converts to Islam (Mohamed & Diamant, 2019). This demographic shift underscores the importance of understanding the unique experiences of African American Muslims, who often navigate complex intersections of race, religion, and identity.

The intersectionality of race and religion also plays a critical role in shaping the mental health outcomes of African American Muslims. Greer (2024) found that African-American-centered spirituality can serve as a buffer against psychological symptoms related to specific forms of racism, suggesting that culturally relevant spiritual practices may mitigate the adverse effects of racial discrimination. However, when spiritual teachings are distorted or misused, they can exacerbate psychological distress, particularly when compounded by experiences of racial trauma. Consequently, recent scholars have emphasized the need to employ intersectional frameworks when examining the experiences of Black Muslim women (Nurein & Iqbal, 2021; Oyewuwo & Walton, 2023). They argue that traditional research methodologies often fail to capture the nuanced realities of this demographic and advocate for approaches that consider the simultaneous impact of race, gender, and religion on their lived experiences.

Moreover, the intersection of racial and spiritual abuse has been identified as a form of 'compound trauma,' wherein individuals experience overlapping systems of oppression that intensify their psychological distress (Ramler, 2023). This concept is particularly relevant for African American Muslims, who may face discrimination within their religious communities due to racial biases, as well as systemic racism in broader society. Such compounded experiences necessitate a comprehensive understanding of how intersecting identities influence mental health outcomes.

In light of these complexities, mental health practitioners and researchers must develop culturally responsive interventions that address the unique needs of African American Muslims. This includes recognizing the role of spiritual abuse in contributing to psychological distress and understanding how racial trauma may moderate this relationship. By adopting intersectional frameworks and culturally attuned approaches, we can better support the mental health and well-being of this marginalized community.

1.1 The Research Problem and Purpose

The problem addressed in this study is how racial trauma intersects with spiritual abuse to impact psychological distress among African American Muslims. While spiritual abuse, the misuse of religious authority to dominate or control, has been linked to long-term psychological harm, including anxiety, depression, and identity fragmentation (Awaad & Riaz, 2022; Rhee, 2024), racial trauma, stemming from systemic discrimination and historical oppression, similarly causes significant psychological distress (Kathawalla & Syed, 2021; Ramler, 2023).

Although both trauma types are recognized independently, research has rarely investigated their combined impact, particularly in marginalized religious groups such as African American Muslims. Existing studies tend to focus on spiritual abuse within predominantly White, Christian contexts, excluding culturally distinct populations and reinforcing gaps in trauma-informed care (Cashwell & Swindle, 2020; Fernández, 2022). This oversight has prevented the development of culturally responsive frameworks that account for the compounding nature of these overlapping traumas.

African American Muslims, comprising approximately 40% of native-born U.S. Muslims, inhabit a unique socio-religious space shaped by both racial and religious marginalization (Pew

Research Center, 2019). Emerging researchers suggest that racial oppression intensifies the psychological toll of spiritual abuse within this community. However, few researchers explore this intersection in depth, leaving those affected vulnerable to misdiagnosis, ineffective therapy, and institutional neglect (Abdalla, 2023; Nsour, 2022).

Without intersectional approaches, mental health practitioners and religious leaders may fail to recognize how these dual forms of trauma function together. This study aimed to fill that gap by examining how racial trauma moderates the relationship between spiritual abuse and psychological distress in African American Muslims, offering a more inclusive, culturally informed understanding of trauma and healing.

The central purpose of this book is to present an integrated, evidence-informed account of how spiritual abuse and racial trauma intersect to shape mental health outcomes among African American Muslims. It aims to translate empirical findings into practical guidance for trauma-informed clinical care, congregational accountability, and community-centered interventions while amplifying survivor voices and advancing an intersectional conceptual model of compound trauma. The argument is reflexive and multidimensional: trauma is treated as psychological, spiritual, and sociopolitical simultaneously, and meaningful healing is framed as requiring interventions that attend to these linked domains rather than to any one in isolation.

The book focuses on three interrelated domains. First, it clarifies the mechanisms and manifestations of spiritual abuse as they appear in Muslim congregational and intra-communal settings, examples include doctrinal weaponization, spiritual gaslighting, and institutional silence, placing those mechanisms in conversation with broader typologies of religious harm. Second, it situates these spiritually injurious dynamics within the wider landscape of racial trauma, demonstrating how anti-Blackness both in U.S. society and within Muslim communities amplifies epistemic exclusion and narrows access to meaningful redress. Third, the book offers practice-oriented directions for clinicians, congregational stakeholders, and policy actors aimed at preventing harm, promoting survivor recovery, and reforming institutional practices; these applied recommendations draw on mixed-methods evidence and survivor testimony to ground reform in both research and lived experience (Ward, 2011).

This work is written for multiple overlapping audiences, each with distinct capacities to respond to the problems documented here. For mental health practitioners such as psychologists, counselors, social workers, and psychiatrists, the book provides culturally and spiritually competent assessment and treatment frameworks for compound traumas that involve spiritual abuse and race-based stress, emphasizing approaches that preserve spiritual resources while addressing trauma (Ortega-Williams et al., 2021; Pargament & Exline, 2020).

For faith leaders and congregational stakeholders: imams, boards, chaplains, and institutional administrators, the book offers evidence-based strategies for accountability, transparent complaint processes, and leadership training designed to reduce the organizational conditions that enable spiritual abuse (Mulvihill et al., 2023; Smith & Freyd, 2014). For survivors and community advocates, the text aims to validate experiences, suggest pathways to reclaim spiritual agency, and provide practical tools for grassroots advocacy and mutual support (Oakley & Humphreys, 2018; Vis & Boynton, 2024).

Finally, for scholars and students, the book advances research on religious harm, racial trauma, and intersectionality by proposing avenues for methodological refinement, culturally grounded measurement, and longitudinal inquiry to more precisely chart causal and temporal dynamics (Crenshaw, 1989; Meyer, 2003). Across these audiences, the book seeks to be both rigorous and praxis-oriented, synthesizing theory, empirical evidence, and first-person narratives to help readers better understand and act on the compounded harms described.

1.2 The Significance of This Research

This study addresses a clear and consequential gap in trauma scholarship by interrogating how spiritual abuse and racial trauma co-occur and jointly shape psychological distress among African American Muslims. Spiritual abuse, using religious authority to control, shame, or silence, can cause long-term psychological harm, including anxiety, depression, and identity issues. Racial trauma from systemic discrimination also creates serious mental-health challenges. However, research on these topics has mostly developed separately rather than together.

The relative separation of these domains has practical consequences: when studies and clinical models treat religious harm and race-based stress as discrete phenomena, they risk overlooking the ways that anti-Blackness, Islamophobia, and intra-communal hierarchies can amplify and transform the psychological impact of spiritually injurious experiences.

The field has a pronounced empirical blind spot with regard to racially minoritized Muslim communities. Much of the extant research on spiritual abuse focuses on White, Christian contexts (Cashwell & Swindle, 2020; Fernández, 2022), producing typologies, measures, and clinical recommendations that may not translate to congregational forms of harm that emerge where race, religious authority, and historical marginalization intersect.

African American Muslims occupy a distinct socio-religious position, one that combines lived experience of anti-Black racism with religious belonging and, for many, conversion narratives, and this positioning shapes both the form and meaning of spiritual harm (Abdalla, 2023; Pew Research Center, 2019). Without targeted inquiry into this population, practitioners risk misdiagnosis, therapeutic approaches that neglect spiritual capital, and institutional reforms that fail to address the racialized mechanisms sustaining abuse (Nsour, 2022).

Theoretically, this study advances trauma theory by integrating Minority Stress Theory and intersectionality to conceptualize compound trauma as a product of interlocking structural forces rather than merely additive stressors (Crenshaw, 1989; Meyer, 2003). Minority Stress Theory foregrounds how identity-linked chronic stressors become embodied and manifest as psychological symptoms, while intersectionality locates those stressors within institutionalized patterns of power that determine whose testimony is believed and which harms are recognized. Applying this integrative lens reveals that spiritual abuse in racially marginalized religious spaces is not only an interpersonal violation but also an expression of institutionalized epistemic exclusion and doctrinal control that may be experienced differently, and more perniciously, by African American congregants.

Methodologically and practically, the study's convergent mixed-methods design and use of Interpretative Phenomenological Analysis (IPA) provide both breadth and depth: quantitative measures allow detection of population-level associations, while qualitative narratives illuminate mechanisms, such as doctrinal weaponization, testimonial silencing, and institutional betrayal, that statistics alone can obscure. This multimodal evidence base enables the development of culturally resonant assessment tools and interventions that preserve spiritual agency while addressing race-based harm and institutional complicity.

Clinically, the study addresses an urgent need for culturally and spiritually competent care that recognizes faith as both a source of resilience and a potential source of harm (Pargament & Exline, 2020). Findings are intended to inform trauma-informed therapeutic approaches that integrate religious literacy with anti-racist practice, helping clinicians avoid inadvertently endorsing the same theological logics or institutional deference that sustain spiritual abuse. For community stakeholders, faith leaders, congregational boards, and advocacy organizations, the research provides evidence to guide accountability measures, transparent complaint processes, and leadership training aimed at preventing abuse while restoring communal trust (Mulvihill et al., 2023; Smith & Freyd, 2014).

In scholarly terms, by centering African American Muslim voices, the research also strengthens the epistemic basis for future longitudinal investigations that can map causal pathways, identify protective community resources, and evaluate institutional reforms in context (Ellis et al., 2022; Ramler, 2023). Finally, the study carries normative significance: it amplifies survivor testimony to validate lived experience, reduce hermeneutical marginalization, and advocate for structural change. In doing so, it moves the conversation about religious harm beyond individual pathology toward accountability, reparative practice, and public-health framing, calling on mental-health systems, faith institutions, and policymakers to respond to compounded harms with interventions that are both justice-oriented and clinically effective.

1.3 Why African American Muslims?

African American Muslims occupy a distinctive social location in the U.S. religious landscape. Although national estimates vary by method, African Americans constitute a substantial proportion of the U.S. Muslim population, roughly 20% overall and approximately 40% of native-born Muslims in some reports, many of whom are converts and maintain distinctive cultural and theological traditions (Pew Research Center, 2019). This demographic reality matters for three reasons.

First, the intersection of race and religion produces unique vulnerabilities. African American Muslims routinely navigate anti-Black racism in society alongside Islamophobia in public life; within some Muslim institutional settings, anti-Black norms and cultural gatekeeping can further marginalize their voices (Al'Uqdah et al., 2019; Ahmad et al., 2024). These dual pressures create layered stressors that standard, race- or religion-centric models often fail to capture.

Second, faith institutions are central to cultural life and coping among many African American communities. Religious involvement can be protective, fostering meaning, social support, and resilience, but it also increases exposure to institutional actors and practices that may inflict harm when authority is abused. When protective resources (e.g., mosque networks, spiritual teachings) simultaneously serve as sources of control or exclusion, the resulting injury can be profound and complex.

Third, African American Muslims are underrepresented in empirical work on religious or spiritual abuse. Much of the literature on spiritual harm focuses on white Christian contexts, or on immigrant Muslim populations, thereby obscuring the culturally specific ways that spiritual abuse operates where race, religious identity, and social marginalization intersect (Ellis et al., 2022; Perry, 2024). This underrepresentation creates both clinical blind spots and gaps in community accountability. The present research intentionally centers African American Muslim experiences to rectify these omissions and to inform culturally consonant interventions.

1.4 Core Concepts: Spiritual Abuse, Racial Trauma, Compound Trauma

Clear definitions are necessary because the terms at the heart of this book, spiritual abuse, racial trauma, and compound trauma, are related but distinct. The definitions used here are grounded in the conceptual and empirical literature reviewed in the dissertation and refined through qualitative interviews with survivors.

Spiritual abuse refers to the misuse of religious authority, doctrine, or communal power to manipulate, control, shame, silence, or otherwise harm individuals in spiritual contexts (Awaad & Riaz, 2022; Oakley et al., 2018). Spiritual abuse may be interpersonal, manifesting in coercive relationships between leaders and congregants, or institutional, embedded in policies, practices, or structures that protect abusers and delegitimize survivors.

Mechanisms commonly identified include doctrinal weaponization (teaching theology in ways that justify control), spiritual gaslighting (undermining a person's spiritual perceptions), enforced conformity, and gendered power dynamics (Daniel, 2019; Johnson & VanVonderen, 1991). In this study, spiritual abuse is operationalized with the Spiritual Harm and Abuse Scale (SHAS) (Koch & Edstrom, 2022), which assesses dimensions such as authoritarian leadership, damaging God-image messaging, and institutional prioritization of reputation over safety.

Racial trauma (RT) refers to the cumulative psychological and physiological consequences of exposure to racism, racial discrimination, and race-based violence, including both direct incidents and vicarious or anticipatory experiences (Cénat, 2023; Williams et al., 2022). Unlike isolated discriminatory acts, racial trauma is conceptualized as chronic, identity-linked stress that undermines a person's sense of safety, belonging, and self-worth, and can produce symptoms analogous to posttraumatic stress

(Harrell, 2000; Muscatell et al., 2022). In the dissertation, RT is measured with the Racial Trauma Scale (RTS), which indexes affective distress, hypervigilance/arousal, avoidance, negative self-cognitions, and somatic reactions.

Compound trauma describes the interactive, mutually reinforcing effects that emerge when two or more identity-based harms co-occur—here, spiritual abuse embedded in religious contexts and race-based traumatic stress. Compound trauma is more than the simple sum of harms; it creates distinctive pathways of injury by altering meaning-making frameworks, restricting access to communal coping resources, and producing epistemic harms that make it difficult to name or seek help. For African American Muslims, compound trauma often manifests as epistemic marginalization (testimony discounted on racial or religious grounds), doctrinal weaponization that resonates differently in racialized settings, and institutional betrayal that closes avenues for redress.

These constructs do not operate in isolation. Spiritual abuse frequently involves epistemic injustice, testimonial or hermeneutical harms that devalue a person's credibility or deny them conceptual resources to interpret their experience (Fricker, 2007). When epistemic injustice is racialized, when African American Muslims' accounts are discounted because of race or perceived lack of theological authority, the consequences are particularly severe, leading to identity fragmentation, loss of spiritual agency, and increased psychological distress. The dissertation's findings indicate robust bivariate associations among SHAS, RTS, and psychological distress and qualitative evidence that these harms often co-occur and operate synergistically rather than as isolated stressors.

1.5 The Methodology, Design, and Nature of the Study

This study employed a convergent mixed-methods design because the phenomena under investigation, spiritual abuse and racial trauma experienced by African American Muslims, are simultaneously measurable social phenomena and deeply subjective, meaning-laden experiences. Mixed-methods approaches combine the analytic advantages of quantitative measurement with the interpretive richness of qualitative inquiry, permitting researchers to identify population-level associations while also explaining the mechanisms, contexts, and lived meanings that animate those associations. The convergent design used here collects quantitative and qualitative data in parallel and integrates them during interpretation, ensuring neither strand is subordinate and both mutually inform a coherent account of compound spiritual–racial harm.

The quantitative strand is a cross-sectional correlational design chosen to estimate prevalence and test relationships among focal constructs, spiritual abuse, racial trauma, and psychological distress, at a single point in time. Cross-sectional correlational methods are appropriate for identifying associations that warrant further causal or longitudinal inquiry, while acknowledging their limits regarding causal inference. Two validated psychometric instruments operationalize the primary constructs: the Spiritual

Harm and Abuse Scale captures experiences of spiritually rooted coercion and doctrinal manipulation, and the Racial Trauma Scale indexes race-related traumatic stress manifestations. These tools permit statistical examination of core research questions, whether spiritual abuse and racial trauma each relate to psychological distress and whether racial trauma alters the strength or form of the spiritual abuse–distress association, while also enabling sensitivity checks for shared variance and measurement overlap.

Complementing the survey data, the qualitative strand uses Interpretative Phenomenological Analysis (IPA) to center participants' sense-making about how spiritual and racial harms are experienced, narrated, and resisted. IPA's idiographic and hermeneutic commitments make it well-suited to explore how structural conditions (e.g., anti-Blackness, doctrinal gatekeeping) are lived and interpreted in personal terms, producing themes such as epistemic marginalization, doctrinal weaponization, and institutional betrayal. IPA was selected because it offers a structured yet interpretive analytic process, bracketing researcher preconceptions, line-by-line coding, and development of Personal Experiential Themes (PETs) and Group Experiential Themes (GETs), which aligns with the study's intersectional theoretical frame (Giorgi, 2009; van Manen, 2016).

Integration is intentional and conceptually driven: quantitative patterns (for example, correlations or regression

21

coefficients) are placed in dialogue with IPA-derived narratives to explain mechanisms and contextual contingencies. Where the survey may indicate a robust association between SHAS scores and psychological distress, IPA excerpts can reveal the organizational practices and theological framings that make spiritual abuse distressing in racially inflected ways; conversely, narrative evidence of epistemic exclusion can prompt re-examination of measurement items for cultural specificity. This dialogical integration strengthens internal validity and triangulation and helps translate statistical associations into actionable understandings for clinicians and community stakeholders.

The research questions and hypotheses are embedded within this mixed-methods logic. RQ1 asks about the relationship between spiritual abuse and psychological distress: the quantitative component tests this relationship statistically using the SHAS and distress indices, while the qualitative component probes how spiritually coercive practices produce proximal stressors and identity disruptions that manifest as distress. RQ2 mirrors this approach for racial trauma: the RTS provides quantification of race-based traumatic symptoms to test association with distress, and IPA uncovers the social and historical contexts through which racialized experiences translate into psychological harm. RQ3 inquires whether racial trauma moderates the spiritual abuse–distress link, which is approached primarily through regression-based interaction testing in the quantitative strand, mindful of multicollinearity and the likelihood that the constructs are entangled. Qualitative narratives are used to interrogate moderation logic by revealing how racialized institutional practices make spiritual abuse more or less harmful in particular contexts. RQ4 is inherently qualitative: IPA explores how African American Muslim participants interpret and give meaning to the co-occurrence of spiritual and racial harm, yielding the thick descriptions necessary to understand pathways to both injury and resilience.

Methodological decisions were shaped by practical and ethical considerations. The convergent mixed-methods design maximizes explanatory power while honoring participants' epistemic authority: quantitative instruments confer comparability and generalizability, and IPA amplifies participant voice and contextual meaning. In short, the study's methodology and design were chosen to fit the complex nature of compound spiritual–racial trauma: to detect patterns across a sample, to explain mechanisms through lived experience, and to integrate both forms of evidence into findings that are scientifically robust and socially relevant.

1.6 Overview of the Mixed-Methods Design

This book is researched and organized utilizing a convergent mixed-methods study (two independent designs integrated into one result) whose value lies not in any single result but in how its dual strands mutually generated a richer, more actionable account of compound spiritual–racial trauma. The integrated orientation shapes the book's structure: quantitative patterns (based on numbers and statistics) indicate scope and co-occurrence, while qualitative narratives furnish mechanism, meaning, and texture. Together, they allow the text to move fluently between population-level claims and the lived realities that give those numbers human and institutional significance, thereby bridging empirical evidence and ethical urgency.

Methodologically, using both strands equally enables the book to interrogate the limits of each mode of inquiry without diminishing either. Statistical models are treated as evidentiary signals rather than final answers; narrative data are treated as explanatory resources rather than anecdotal exceptions. These dialectic yields distinctive contributions to theory: it reframes spiritual abuse and racial trauma as mutually constitutive processes unfolding across structural, institutional, relational, and embodied levels, and it provides the empirical and hermeneutic material needed to articulate an integrated model of compound trauma that guides future multilevel research and practice.

Practically, the mixed-methods foundation enhances the book's utility for multiple audiences. For clinicians and mental-health practitioners, integrating psychometric indicators with immersive participant accounts yields assessment heuristics and case-sensitive formulations that acknowledge both spiritual resources and race-based vulnerabilities, thereby supporting culturally and spiritually competent care.

For congregational leaders and institutional stakeholders, the combination of prevalence evidence and qualitative descriptions of organizational patterns provides a basis for designing complaint pathways, accountability structures, and training informed by both measurable risk and the lived experiences of marginalized congregants. For scholars, the mixed evidence points to methodological innovations, such as iterative instrument development informed by narrative themes and multilevel modeling that respects cultural specificity, while also inviting theoretical refinement of minority-stress and intersectional frameworks.

Finally, the book treats the mixed-methods enterprise as a model of ethical scholarship in contexts of epistemic vulnerability. Centering survivors' interpretive authority alongside quantitative indicators resists reductionism and mitigates the risk that marginalized experiences will be subsumed under generic diagnostic labels. In doing so, the study exemplifies how empirical rigor and interpretive humility can be combined to produce research that is both scientifically credible and socially accountable, an approach that, as the chapters that follow demonstrate, is uniquely suited to capturing the complex realities of spiritual abuse and racial trauma in racially marginalized faith communities.

1.7 Roadmap for Readers

This book is designed as a practical map and companion for anyone seeking to understand, intervene in, and heal from the layered harms of spiritual abuse and racial trauma. It is organized to progress from conceptual framing to evidence synthesis, then to practical application. The reader may move through a full arc from theory to practice or jump to the sections most relevant to their need. Begin with the framing chapters to learn the integrated lens of Minority Stress and Intersectionality, which orients the whole work and helps readers new to religious harm situate clinical symptoms or institutional patterns within broader power structures. Next, the reader may proceed into the contextual literature to access concise syntheses of how spirituality can both protect and wound, and gather annotated references that clinicians and educators can use to deepen their practice.

The central empirical section offers transparent accounts of the study's approach and integrative logic; scholars and advanced practitioners will find the methodological detail, joint displays, and analytic reflections useful for designing future research or adapting measures. The analytic chapters are interposed with findings that trace the mechanisms of compound harm, how toxic theology, patriarchal authority, epistemic exclusion, and institutional betrayal translate doctrinal norms into psychospiritual injury, which congregational leaders, policy advocates, and community organizers can use to identify specific levers for reform.

The applied portion of the book translates evidence into actionable tools for healing and prevention: clinical guidance for trauma-informed, spiritually competent care; screening prompts and interview language for assessment; concrete complaint-process templates and leadership training modules for institutions; and community-level strategies for mutual aid, survivor support, and restorative accountability. Later chapters expand on measurement and future research directions, offering pathways for longitudinal, community-engaged, and multilevel studies that can refine interventions and policy. The appendices gather ready-to-use resources, interview protocols, the SHAS and RTS instruments, integration templates, sample congregational policies, and curated lists of culturally competent clinical and community supports, enabling readers to move immediately from learning to implementation.

Use this book as a healing resource by reading the narrative vignettes and using the practical tools that validate survivor experiences and offer concrete recovery pathways. Use it as an educational text by assigning foundational chapters and case materials in training settings, as a leadership guide by applying the institutional analyses and policy templates to reform governance and complaint procedures, and as a practical handbook by adapting the screening items, referral networks, and trauma-informed protocols for clinical intake and community advocacy. Throughout, the work centers on survivor testimony and ethical responsibility. Understanding the problem is only the first step; the primary aim is to equip readers to act: restore spiritual agency, demand institutional accountability, and foster healing practices that honor both faith and the dignity of those harmed.

1.8 Definitions of Key Terms

African American Muslims

A diverse population of Black individuals in the United States who identify as Muslim. They comprise approximately 40% of native-born U.S. Muslims and occupy a distinct socio-religious position shaped by intersecting racial and religious marginalization.

Cultural Marginalization

Cultural Marginalization refers to the ongoing exclusion of minority cultural identities and worldviews from dominant societal narratives and institutions, often resulting in diminished access to power, representation, and resources.

Epistemic Injustice

Epistemic injustice involves the devaluation or dismissal of an individual's knowledge, experiences, or credibility, particularly in contexts where they are marginalized due to their identity or beliefs.

Intersectional Harm

Intersectional Harm describes the layered and interacting forms of discrimination individuals face when multiple marginalized identities—such as race, gender, and religion—overlap.

Intersection of Spiritual Abuse and Racial Trauma

Intersection of Spiritual Abuse and Racial Trauma refers to the compounded psychological and emotional harm experienced when spiritual abuse occurs within contexts already shaped by racialized trauma, leading to intensified distress and complex barriers to healing, particularly for African American Muslims.

Islamophobia

Islamophobia refers to the irrational fear, hatred, or prejudice against Islam and Muslims, often expressed through discriminatory policies, social exclusion, and violence.

Mechanisms of Spiritual Abuse

Mechanisms of Spiritual Abuse are the specific tactics or structures through which spiritual abuse is enacted. These include, but are not limited to, toxic theology, patriarchal power structures, epistemic injustice, coercive control, doctrinal manipulation, enforced conformity, and the use of shame, fear, or guilt to suppress individual autonomy or dissent.

Marginalization

Marginalization is the social process of "othering" by which certain groups are pushed to the edges of society, denied access to resources, rights, or opportunities, and rendered socially invisible or devalued.

Patriarchal Control / Structures

Patriarchal Control or Structures are social and institutional systems that uphold male dominance and prioritize power primarily within male circles, and restrict women's voices and marginalized groups. In religious settings, these structures can enable spiritual abuse by concentrating authority and reinforcing gender-based control.

Spiritual Gaslighting

Spiritual gaslighting involves manipulating individuals into doubting their spiritual perceptions, beliefs, or experiences, often by using religious doctrine or authority to undermine their credibility or sanity.

Religious Trauma

Religious trauma encompasses the lasting psychological and emotional harm caused by religious teachings, institutions, or leaders, primarily when rooted in control, fear, or shame.

Toxic Theology

Toxic theology refers to religious teachings or interpretations that promote fear, shame, control, or exclusion, often contributing to psychological harm and spiritual confusion.

Systemic Marginalization / Racism

Systemic Marginalization or racism refers to the pervasive operation of policies, practices, and institutional structures that maintain racial inequality and exclusion, often manifesting as disparities in health, housing, education, and the justice system.

Chapter 2:

Theoretical Lenses: Minority Stress and Intersectionality

This chapter develops the conceptual scaffolding for understanding how spiritual abuse and racial trauma cooperate to produce compounded psychological and spiritual harm for African American Muslims. Rather than treating spiritual abuse as an isolated interpersonal pathology or racial trauma as a discrete sociopolitical exposure, the chapter argues that these phenomena must be analyzed through theories that foreground chronic identity-linked stress and intersecting systems of power.

I begin with Minority Stress Theory to clarify the psychosocial mechanisms through which identity-based stress produces harm. I then elaborate Intersectionality Theory to ground structural analyses of how race, religion, and gender interlock. Next, I outline complementary frameworks, institutional betrayal, coercive control, shame theory, and epistemic injustice that illuminate specific pathways through which congregational practices translate into psychospiritual injury. Finally, I synthesize these perspectives into an integrated model of compound spiritual–racial trauma and discuss the implications this model holds for research, clinical practice, and communal accountability.

2.1 Minority Stress Theory: Distal and Proximal Stressors

Minority Stress Theory (MST) provides an essential starting point for understanding why identity-linked exposures matter for health. Originally articulated by Meyer (2003) to explain disparities among sexual minorities, MST posits that members of stigmatized groups face additional, socially generated stressors over and above general life strain; these stressors are chronic, tied to identity, and operate through both external events (distal stressors) and internal processes (proximal stressors).

Distal stressors include overt discrimination, exclusion, and violence; proximal stressors include anticipatory vigilance, concealment, and internalized stigma. Crucially, MST reframes mental health disparities as rational responses to hostile social environments rather than as intrapsychic deficits (Frost & Meyer, 2023).

Applied to African American Muslims, MST helps explain how the daily navigation of anti-Black racism, Islamophobia, and intra-religious marginalization generates an ongoing allostatic load that predisposes to anxiety, depression, and trauma-like symptomatology. Where religious institutions are trusted sources of meaning and social support, the misuse of religious authority, spiritual abuse, becomes another distal stressor with proximal reverberations. For example, doctrinal weaponization or institutional silence can produce anticipatory fear (Will speaking up lead to spiritual exclusion?) and internalized shame (Did I cause this suffering by failing spiritually?), both of which match MST's proximal stressor category and have demonstrated associations with poorer psychological outcomes.

Recent refinements of MST underscore its applicability to multiple marginalized groups. Rather than treating minority statuses as additive, scholars emphasize temporal, contextual, and relational dynamics, how multiple forms of social exclusion converge across the lifespan to shape stress trajectories. This nuance is essential: African American Muslims' experiences of stress are rarely reducible to either race or religion alone; they are produced in the daily negotiations across social settings where both identities are salient.

2.2 Intersectionality: Race, Religion, Gender

Intersectionality theory, rooted in Black feminist legal scholarship (Crenshaw, 1989), offers an essential structural complement to MST. While MST emphasizes psychosocial processes, intersectionality highlights the power structures that create those processes. Intersectionality argues that systems like white supremacy, patriarchy, and religious authority not only accumulate but also interact to produce distinctly different forms of marginalization.

For African American Muslims, intersectionality directs analytic attention to how anti-Blackness operates inside Muslim institutions, through racialized leadership hierarchies, cultural gatekeeping, and theological delegitimization, and how patriarchal religious structures reproduce gendered subordination. These interlocking systems shape who is believed, who has interpretive authority, and who can safely claim victimhood. For example, a Black Muslim woman raising concerns about marital abuse may face a triple bind: racial discounting of her theological authority, patriarchal minimization of her complaint, and institutional protection of male leadership (Abdalla, 2023; Lateef & Umarji, 2022). Intersectionality thus explains why institutional responses are patterned and why certain survivors bear greater barriers to recognition and support.

Methodologically, intersectionality challenges researchers to use methods that demonstrate how different factors interact, rather than merely add up across levels (structural, institutional, interpersonal). It also demands that we remain humble, as each community's beliefs and experiences are unique and cannot be fully understood with general research tools. This insight underpins the mixed-methods approach that grounds this book: quantitative measures identify correlations and prevalence, while qualitative work reveals how systemic power is experienced, narrated, and resisted in context.

2.3 Complementary Theories

To show how institutions and relationships turn structural power into personal harm, several helpful theories explain how this harm happens. Smith and Freyd's (2014) concept of institutional betrayal describes how organizations on which individuals depend can fail to prevent harm or even increase it by silencing complainants, protecting reputations, or disciplining those who speak out. Institutional betrayal not only prolongs trauma but also undermines help-seeking by eroding trust in structures that otherwise offer care (Andresen et al., 2019). In religious settings, institutional betrayal often protects community leaders and influential members rather than protecting those who are being harmed, thereby converting individual abuses into systemic harms.

Coercive control theory, developed in domestic violence literature, highlights how sustained patterns of surveillance, isolation, threat, and manipulation enact a durable form of domination (Lohmann et al., 2024). Within faith communities, such control may be spiritualized, framed as obedience to God or the protection of community purity, making it hard to resist morally. The doctrinal weaponization described in Chapter 1 becomes intelligible in these terms: spiritual authority is employed to demand submission, thereby normalizing coercion under sacred language.

Shame plays a central role in many spiritually abusive situations. Unlike guilt, which targets specific actions, shame attacks the self and erodes a person's sense of worth. Doctrinal narratives that cast suffering as divine punishment or disagreement as moral failure turn theology into a weapon, producing deep shame that stops people from speaking out and encourages self-blame (Shi et al., 2021). Shame works both inside the individual and in social contexts: it isolates survivors and undermines the credibility of their requests for help.

Miranda Fricker's (2007) work on epistemic injustice explains how marginalized people are often not believed (testimonial injustice) or don't have the words to describe their own harm (hermeneutical injustice).

In religious spaces with racial hierarchies, African American Muslims are often not believed, and the community lacks the right language to talk about spiritual harm in ways that fit their culture. This double bind makes it even harder for people to be recognized, supported by others, or receive help to repair the harm (Rekis, 2023).

These frameworks interlock: controlling behavior often occurs in institutions that betray trust; shame keeps people silent and allows institutions to hide problems; and injustice in knowledge both causes and strengthens institutional power. Together, these show how macro systems of oppression often cause severe personal suffering.

2.4 An Integrated Model

An integrated model of compound spiritual–racial trauma foregrounds how multiple levels of power and meaning-making combine to produce distinct patterns of harm among American minority religious communities. At the broadest level, structural forces, white supremacy, patriarchy, and established religious hierarchies determine who gains access to authority, which theology is promoted, and whose experiences count as credible within both society and faith institutions. These broad conditions are not meaningless backdrops but shapers of institutional power and determinants of the rules by which we understand the factors that make certain forms of spiritual suffering visible and others invisible.

These large patterns show up in religious groups and organizations, where leadership rules, strict beliefs, and secretive policies turn unequal power into daily life. When institutions protect wrongdoers, silence complaints, and care more about their reputation than survivors, personal mistreatment becomes an organization-wide problem. In these places, religious language can be used to justify controlling behavior and make it hard to hold institutions accountable.

At the interpersonal level, these institutional and structural dynamics shape relationships within congregations. Power manifests through coercive control, spiritual gaslighting, and testimonial discounting, tactics that directly create proximal stressors identified by Minority Stress Theory, including shame, identity fragmentation, and hypervigilance. These relational processes are not isolated events but patterned interactions that mirror and reinforce the broader systems around them: who is listened to, who is assumed to be knowledgeable, and who is regarded as deviant or expendable.

This complex process leads to psychological and physical effects, such as anxiety, depression, loss of trust in spiritual knowledge, trouble regulating the body, and withdrawal from others. These issues arise from repeated harm and from having fewer ways to cope when the community itself is part of the problem.

A key part of this model is feedback: when survivors feel distress and withdraw, they are less able to challenge harmful institutional practices, allowing these harmful norms to grow stronger. Since much of the harm is justified with religious language and seen as a spiritual duty, the model shows how people lose both their sense of safety and their ability to speak and be heard in their communities.

This complex connection also affects research methods. If racial trauma is treated as just another factor in the link between spiritual abuse and distress, it can lead to misunderstanding, because these issues are deeply connected and influence each other at all levels. The strong overlap found between spiritual abuse and racial trauma in this study supports the idea that they are tightly linked, not separate causes. So, researchers should use approaches that consider the full complexity, focusing on how different forces interact, rather than trying to isolate a single cause amid overlapping social, institutional, and personal factors.

2.5 Implications for Research

Clinicians working with African American Muslim clients should adopt trauma-informed, spiritually literate, and race-attentive approaches. Assessment should screen for spiritual abuse alongside race-based stressors, and interventions should address moral-epistemic injury, restoring spiritual agency and testimony, alongside symptom reduction. Cultural humility and collaboration with community-based supports are essential, as is clinician awareness of institutional dynamics that may impede referral or protection.

Based on the research findings, congregations play a role in allowing spiritual abuse and discrimination within their own communities. It also highlights how Islam's worldwide presence can interact with local customs, which often become part of religious teachings and practices (Aziz, 2022). Research should examine how congregations create and reinforce power structures that support the control of religious authority and racial exclusion. It's important to focus on how the community views accountability and solutions, rather than treating harm as merely an individual problem (Choudhury, 2022). Comparing how similar religious beliefs or practices change in different cultures can show whether abuse comes from theology, cultural traditions, or their overlap with racial hierarchies in Muslim communities.

Researchers should explore congregational responses to allegations of spiritual abuse, including mechanisms of silence, minimization, or reform, and how these responses differ across diasporic networks and national settings; such attention will illuminate institutional barriers to survivor safety and to equitable treatment of intra-racial minorities. Additionally, research scholarship should partner with community members to find accountability practices that fit the culture and to test programs that make congregations more open, fair, and protective of marginalized people. This way, the research will be both thorough and helpful for communities wanting real change.

Congregational reform must move beyond simple individual leader training to structural changes: transparent complaint processes, survivor-centered investigative procedures, redistribution of interpretive authority, and mechanisms for institutional courage that prioritize safety over reputation (Smidt et al., 2023). Because harms are often legitimized through theological language, accountability work should include theological education that reclaims religious resources for emancipation rather than control.

Taken together, Minority Stress Theory and Intersectionality, augmented by institutional betrayal, coercive control, shame theory, and epistemic injustice, offer a robust, multi-level theoretical framework for understanding compound spiritual–racial trauma. This architecture explains why spiritual abuse in African American Muslim contexts cannot be disentangled from race or gendered power, why institutional reform is as necessary as individual therapy, and why research must be both methodologically plural and ethically grounded. The chapters that follow apply and extend this theoretical frame to empirical findings, clinical interventions, and actionable strategies for communal repair.

Part II

Literature and Context

Chapter 3:

Spirituality, Religion, and the Dual Functions of Faith

Spiritual life sits at the center of many people's efforts to survive, make sense of suffering, and find a sense of belonging. For African American Muslims in particular, faith often serves as both a compass and a community. It provides moral meaning, historical memory, and practical resources to endure structural exclusion. Yet these same spiritual structures can be contested ground, sites where authority, doctrine, and community norms either protect or harm. This chapter examines that tension. It treats spirituality neither as completely positive nor as the main cause of problems, but as something shaped by institutions, power, and cultural meanings that needs to be understood within these contexts.

Framing the discussion this way requires attending to two complementary questions. First, how does spirituality operate as a resource? What are the pathways through which religious belief, ritual, and community foster resilience, narrative repair, and social support in the face of adversity? Second, when and how do the same mechanisms become instruments of harm, what theological, relational, and organizational processes transform spiritual resources into sources of shame, control, and epistemic marginalization? Answering these questions demands a combined approach that links psychological and cultural perspectives, centers real-life experiences, and is based on research and theory about religion, trauma, and minority stress. The sections that follow explore these complementary dimensions. First, spirituality's resilient capacities; then, the pathways by which faith can be turned to harm; next, the institutional contexts that mediate both outcomes; and finally, comparative lessons from other traditions that highlight both risks and possibilities for repair.

3.1 Spirituality as a Resource

For many people, spirituality and religious participation are foundational resources for coping, sense-making, and community support, especially in communities that have historically faced structural marginalization and exclusion. Across disciplines, research demonstrates that spiritual frameworks help people make sense of suffering, find new purpose, and build social support, which, in turn, reduces emotional and psychological distress following hardship (Bonelli & Koenig, 2013).

In trauma-informed terms, spirituality often operates as a meaning-making engine: it offers narratives that integrate loss into a larger story, provides beliefs about suffering that can buffer despair, and supplies rituals and community practices that regulate emotion and re-establish social bonds (Currier et al., 2024; Walsh, 2017). These processes have been linked empirically to posttraumatic growth, improved emotion regulation, and greater perseverance in the face of prolonged hardship (Ozcan et al., 2021).

When specifically applied to African American Muslim communities, the protective functions of spirituality take on culturally unique forms. Religious traditions like Islam can serve as a source of cultural continuity and collective memory for Black Americans, grounding identity in theological narratives that oppose racial hierarchy and uphold human dignity. This culturally rooted spirituality enhances resilience by offering a shared language of resistance and a range of practices, such as communal prayer, mutual aid, and spiritual mentorship, that foster social support and meaning reconstruction (Gillum et al., 2006).

Empirical work demonstrates that therapy that includes spiritual and cultural practices can help lower depression and trauma symptoms and improve coping. These results match other studies, which find that using religion to cope, seeking spiritual support, viewing suffering as meaningful, and trusting in the one caring God of the universe, all lead to better mental health in many diverse cultures.

At the level of lived experience, faith can transform marginalization into a narrative of collective endurance rather than personal failure (Ward, 2011). Religious identity offers members of minoritized groups an interpretive lens that reframes discriminatory encounters as part of a broader structural injustice, thereby externalizing blame and protecting the self from internalized stigma. This externalization aligns with Minority Stress Theory, which says that social stress can become part of a person's inner experience. Spiritual and community support can help reduce this stress by offering new ways to understand it and a sense of belonging.

For many African American Muslims, theology and communal narratives cultivate both a language through which to name racialized pain and a set of collective practices that re-stitch social trust when broader society is hostile. It is also important to acknowledge that these protective mechanisms are not uniformly available to all members within a community. Access to spiritually affirming guidance and supportive institutional responses depends on the presence of accountable leadership, inclusive Islamic interpretive traditions, and social networks that validate survivors' epistemic claims.

Where those resources are present, where religious communities practice what has been termed institutional courage, spirituality can be a powerful vehicle for healing. Conversely, when principled leadership is absent, communities become harsh and oppressive, protecting reputation rather than people. The result is that the potential for harm grows, and the same spiritual structures that could foster strength and resilience become sources of further harm.

3.2 When Faith Harms

The beneficial aspects of spirituality coexist uneasily with its potential to cause harm. Throughout a broad range of literature, scholars have documented how religious doctrine, authority, and rituals can be weaponized to cause psychological harm, which has been called spiritual abuse, religious trauma, or toxic theology (Daniel, 2019; Johnson & VanVonderen, 1991). The ways in which faith is turned into harm are complex and occur at doctrinal, intimate relationship, and institutional levels.

Doctrinally, fundamentalist, authoritarian, or perfectionist interpretations often equate suffering with moral or divine testing or punishment, where congregants are encouraged to be patient with their mistreatment. This theological framing is often applied even in cases of domestic violence, where ongoing shame and identity erosion are strong symptoms of trauma, depression, anxiety, and identity fragmentation (Panchuk, 2018).

Relationally, spiritual authority structures that grant excessive moral jurisdiction to spouses or community leaders create conditions ripe for coercive control. Husbands or leaders who claim exclusive access to religious knowledge or divine endorsement of their position can delegitimize disagreement and enforce compliance by misapplying sacred texts, threats of spiritual exclusion and punishment, labeling dissenters as sinful, or invoking divine condemnation to silence critique.

These dynamics mirror broader models of coercive control and betrayal trauma, whereby dependency on a trusted authority is exploited to produce and conceal abuse. In such contexts, victims may experience a profound rupture in their relationship to both community, household, and faith, producing what psychology scholars characterize as spiritual struggles that compound psychological distress (Pargament & Exline, 2021).

Institutional pathways worsen these harms. Institutions prioritizing reputation over accountability and normalizing the suppression of complaints create systemic disenfranchisement of survivors. Institutional betrayal not only extends exposure to harm but also weakens opportunities for social repair: when complaints are dismissed, poorly investigated, or redirected into spiritually framed admonitions, victims have fewer resources to process trauma and more reasons to withdraw or blame themselves (Mulvihill et al., 2023; Smith & Freyd, 2014). The qualitative interviews from this research documented multiple cases where doctrinal language was used to label survivors' testimony as immoral or divisive, effectively shutting down social avenues for redress and creating identity confusion and physical symptoms among those affected.

Moreover, spiritual abuse's psychological footprints are broad. Survivors often report symptoms that parallel, and sometimes meet criteria for, trauma-related disorders: intrusive recollections, hypervigilance, avoidance behaviors, and dysregulated affect. Yet these clinical manifestations are frequently accompanied by domain-specific spiritual sequelae, damaged God-image, loss of spiritual trust, and moral-epistemic injury that standard psychiatric measures can overlook (Stone, 2013; Winell, 2011).

Moral-epistemic injury, a concept increasingly used to describe the erosion of one's ability to trust their own moral and knowledge judgments, captures the particular cruelty of spiritual abuse. The harm affects not only the mind and body but also the individual's sense of knowing and being known by their Lord (Ramler, 2023).

3.3 Religious Institutions

Religious institutions have mixed effects in community life. They can be sources of support, moral guidance, and practical help, places where people mourn together, find opportunities, and build identity. But they can also cause harm. Rigid hierarchies, unclear channels for reporting problems, and treating leaders as unquestionable can allow abuse to go unchallenged or remain hidden.

For Black communities in particular, the faith tradition has long been a source of social resilience and political mobilization. Churches provide emotional support, leadership training, and organized space to resist and recover from the harms of systemic racism. African American Muslim masjids and community centers serve similar purposes, with worship, education, and mutual aid helping people cope with marginalization. At the same time, the same strengths that hold communities together, strict hierarchies, closed decision-making, and reverence for leaders, can make it hard to report problems, protect victims, or challenge abuse. Cultural pressures to keep issues private can further silence members and shield offenders. The result is a complex mix: faith institutions that give meaning, support, and tools for collective action can also, without accountability, enable harm and conceal wrongdoing.

The scholarship on institutional complacency, developed from analyses of the Catholic clergy scandals and extended into other faith contexts, reveals predictable organizational patterns: prioritizing institutional reputation, gatekeeping information, and implementing procedures that discourage reporting. In Muslim contexts, these dynamics can be amplified by intra-religious racial hierarchies and cultural gatekeeping that diminish African American voices, increasing epistemic silencing.

Institutional responses, or failures of response, have measurable psychological consequences. Where institutions respond with accountability, survivors report lower symptom severity and greater willingness to remain engaged in community life. Where institutions are lackadaisical or treat disclosures casually and without urgency, survivors experience enhanced distress and a sustained erosion of trust. Moreover, the kind of support survivors get depends on the institution. If the institution is willing to change, survivors may heal through help from the community or by reclaiming their faith. But if the institution betrays them, survivors might have to turn to outside therapy or leave religion completely (Captari et al., 2024; Vis & Boynton, 2024).

Understanding these institutional dynamics, therefore, requires moving beyond individual pathology to examine organizational incentives and structures, as well as the cultural scripts that determine whose testimonies count. Institutional reform efforts that put members' safety first, gain community trust, and establish transparent processes, which have been described in the literature as institutional courage capable of reducing long-term harms (Adams Clark et al., 2024; Goertzen & Yancey, 2025). The point is not to denigrate religious institutions wholesale but to recognize that the same structures that enable care can, when unchecked, become engines of harm.

3.4 The Psychological Sequelae of Spiritual Abuse

The psychological sequelae of spiritual abuse have been widely recognized in the literature as both profound and enduring, particularly among African American Muslim communities, where intersecting racial and religious marginalization compounds the trauma experienced (Abdalla, 2023; Alcalá & Sharif, 2018; Alvidrez & Tabor, 2021; Awaad & Riaz, 2020). A range of studies have established that spiritual abuse results in long-lasting emotional and cognitive harm. The authors of scholarship outlined in separate research findings observed that survivors of spiritual abuse often report chronic feelings of shame, remorse, diminished self-worth, and identity dysfunction symptoms that persist even after individuals have removed themselves from abusive religious contexts.

The trauma associated with spiritual abuse becomes particularly acute when it induces a crisis of faith, compelling individuals to reassess their moral framework, life purpose, and value systems. Doyle (2006) referred to this as 'soul murder,' a term that describes the existential devastation caused by spiritual abuse.

Existing literature suggests that theological manipulation and institutional practices play a significant role in deepening psychological harm. Researchers of Hollier et al. (2022) and scholar Marianne Moyaert (2019) noted that within minority communities, spiritual abuse is frequently enabled by patriarchal systems and epistemic injustice, structures that systematically silence dissenting voices and invalidate individual spiritual experiences. Scholars Al'Uqdah et al. (2019) and Ahmad et al. (2024) further demonstrated that such manipulation causes internalized guilt and impairs one's ability to distinguish genuine spiritual guidance from coercive control. Several studies have also drawn parallels between spiritual abuse and symptoms of PTSD. The authors of Panchuk (2024) and Stone (2013) documented symptoms such as chronic anxiety, hypervigilance, and pervasive distrust of religious institutions, noting that these responses are consistent with trauma-based pathology.

For African American Muslims, the effects of spiritual abuse are often compounded by systemic racism or Islamophobia

(Bassioni & Langrehr, 2021). McLaughlin and company (2022) added that Islamophobic narratives contribute to self-stigma and discourage individuals from seeking mental health support, thereby increasing their vulnerability to chronic psychological dysfunction. This is particularly relevant for African American Muslims, who, according to Bolouri (2022), Rippy and Newman (2024), and Tineo et al. (2021), frequently experience conflict between their religious identity and the racialized expectations imposed upon them both within and outside of their Islamic faith communities.

Speaking more broadly, the literature on religion and mental health provides a critical context for understanding these dynamics. Pargament and Lomax (2013) offered a comprehensive review of the complex relationship between religiosity and mental health, acknowledging the dual role of religion as both a source of healing and a potential contributor to psychological harm. Their research underscores the need to assess religious engagement within therapeutic contexts, especially when that engagement has been shaped by abuse or coercion. Gomez et al. (2021) and Panchuk (2018) advocate for trauma-informed and culturally responsive interventions that prioritize survivor agency and challenge harmful theological constructs.

Similarly, researchers Karaman and Christian (2020) advocate for comprehensive reforms that incorporate theological inquiry, gender equity, and institutional accountability as essential components in fostering healing and resilience.

3.5 Coping and Healing Mechanisms

Recent scholarship on coping and healing from spiritual abuse underscores the need for healing frameworks that are not only trauma-informed but also culturally responsive and spiritually attuned. Heath and Cutrer-Párraga (2020) argue that recovery from the compounded effects of spiritual and racial trauma cannot be separated from the broader socio-cultural and religious environments in which harm occurs.

Trauma-informed care models, though foundational, remain insufficient when they fail to address the intersecting racial, cultural, and spiritual identities of survivors. This limitation is especially significant for African American Muslims, who often face multiple layers of marginalization: anti-Black racism, anti-Western discrimination, Islamophobia, and, for some, gender discrimination. In these contexts, healing requires treatment that must account for the multiple, interlocking forms of oppression.

The trauma psychology literature emphasizes that cultural humility is a cornerstone of effective treatment interventions. Plaisime et al. (2023) identify cultural humility as more than a clinical stance; it is an ongoing practice of contextual sensitivity that resists reproducing power dynamics. This is crucial for African American Muslims, whose experiences of spiritual abuse are often compounded by histories of knowledge exclusion and institutional mistrust, both within religious communities and within mental healthcare systems. Without culturally humble approaches, survivors risk encountering further silencing and re-traumatization.

Ranjbar et al. (2020) further emphasize that therapy should incorporate survivors' spiritual beliefs. Ignoring the role of faith in healing not only alienates individuals but also deprives them of one of the most powerful resources for resilience and meaning-making. This is especially important for African American Muslims, whose spirituality often offers a framework for understanding suffering, building resistance, and fostering community solidarity. Recent studies show that faith-based coping, when acknowledged and supported, can serve as a protective factor against psychological distress, particularly in communities facing multiple forms of oppression.

Vis and Boynton (2024) add that healing spiritual trauma in minority communities needs practices that help survivors take back their religious identities and stand up to controlling authority. For African American Muslims, this can mean separating Islam's message of freedom from patriarchal ideas pushed by male-dominated leaders or institutions. These kinds of restorative practices fit with intersectional healing methods, which understand that true empowerment means facing and challenging the systems of hierarchy, racism, sexism, and Islamophobia that allow abuse to happen.

Recent research supports these points. Captari and Worthington (2024) and Çınaroğlu (2024) show that interventions tailored to spiritual and cultural needs help minoritized groups feel better and become more resilient. Hodge et al. (2024) and Stanton (2020) add that therapies that address both racial and religious identities can reduce trauma's harmful effects for African American Muslims. They also help practitioners better serve this unique community by focusing on respect and cultural understanding. In contrast, methods that ignore these identities may make it harder for survivors to find the ideas or spiritual support they need to understand their experiences.

Taken together, this growing body of research affirms that effective healing from spiritual abuse among African American Muslims requires integrative, intersectional frameworks that center survivors' cultural and spiritual realities. Healing in these contexts cannot be reduced to symptom management alone. Instead, it must involve restoring dignity, affirming epistemic agency, and creating space for survivors to reengage spirituality as a resource for liberation rather than control.

3.6 Comparative Perspectives Across Traditions

Comparative research on spiritual abuse reveals both common patterns and tradition-specific traits. Across Christian, Jewish, Muslim, and other faiths, scholars identify similar mechanisms, doctrinal manipulation, clericalism, and institutional protectionism, indicating that spiritual abuse is not exclusive to any one religion but a result of unchecked authority wherever it occurs. For example, studies on sexual abuse by Catholic clergy show that institutions often hide the truth and treat church leaders as sacred; evangelical groups have been criticized for strict leadership and control through spiritual means; similar issues happen in other traditions with strong or top-down leaders whose power goes unchecked and is not held accountable.

At the same time, each tradition's theological vocabularies and governance structures shape how abuse is rationalized and contested. In some evangelical contexts, for instance, doctrines of submission and prophetic authority may be invoked to reframe dissent as spiritual failure, whereas in Muslim settings, specific interpretive debates about scriptural authority, legal tradition, and cultural practice influence the boundaries of coercion and resistance. Cultural and racial dynamics further infect these processes: minority communities within a given faith may experience distinct forms of epistemic exclusion and cultural marginalization that are invisible in majority populations' discussions of spiritual harm.

Comparative perspectives also shed light on recovery paths that are both universal and specific. Narrative reconstruction, ritual re-engagement, and community healing practices, tools common to many traditions, have been shown to be therapeutic across different contexts. However, the content and process of reclaiming faith usually depend on the religious rules observed in each tradition: some religions offer strong arguments against strict control and new interpretations of their sacred scripture, even when such interpretations support the oppressed, while others lack these resources and need help from outside supporters and therapy.

For African American Muslim communities, comparing different experiences emphasizes how crucial it is to consider both race and religion to better understand harm and healing. The complex nature of Black Muslim identity, often blending African American cultural history, stories of converting to Islam, and Islamic beliefs, creates unique ways of being resilient but also faces specific challenges when racism within the community or male-dominated religious views intersect with wider society's anti-Black attitudes. Comparing different approaches shows that interventions should respect faith and pay attention to race:

combining religious renewal with anti-racist actions and linking community changes with care that understands trauma.

In short, spirituality can both heal and harm, and these effects are neither separate nor equal. Faith can provide strong protection, but it can also be undermined by twisted beliefs, controlling leaders, and institutional betrayal. Comparing different traditions helps reveal common patterns and unique cultural differences, guiding reforms in religious teachings, organizations, and healthcare. The following chapters will demonstrate how these issues appear in the African American Muslim communities studied here, and how survivors, healthcare workers, and communities have addressed both harm and healing.

Summary

The growing body of research on spiritual abuse consistently identifies it as a distinct form of psychological and relational harm rooted in the misuse of religious authority to manipulate belief, suppress autonomy, and enforce compliance. Converging findings from both qualitative and quantitative studies demonstrate how spiritual authority can be weaponized through guilt induction, social isolation, or theological manipulation.

These mechanisms are often hidden within trusted religious institutions, making them harder to recognize and oppose. Scholars agree that spiritual abuse leads to serious psychological effects, such as identity confusion, anxiety, complex trauma, and cognitive dissonance, as survivors struggle to reconcile their personal faith with experiences of betrayal.

However, disagreement arises around the role of religion itself. While some studies stress that spiritual frameworks can foster resilience and meaning, others warn that distorted or authoritarian views can cause harm. This conflict shows a key challenge in treatment: effective recovery depends on telling apart helpful from harmful aspects of faith. Additionally, different forms of spiritual abuse are more frequently recognized, including institutional abuse embedded in organizational doctrine and the use of spirituality to justify coercive control in intimate partner violence. These findings demonstrate both how spiritual language can be adapted across different contexts and the importance of developing more detailed definitions.

Despite these advances, notable gaps still exist. Most empirical research has concentrated on white, Christian-majority settings, which narrows generalizability and risks excluding religious and racial minorities. African American Muslims, in particular, are largely absent from the literature despite experiencing compounded vulnerabilities at the intersection of anti-Black racism, Islamophobia, and patriarchal religious authority.

Limited but emerging studies suggest that African American Muslims frequently experience theological silencing, racial exclusion within Islamic spaces, and authoritarian interpretations that reproduce racial hierarchies. These dynamics point to a layered form of spiritual abuse that is distinct from both immigrant Muslim experiences and Black Christian traditions.

Convergence across trauma, feminist, and religious studies literature confirms the severity and complexity of spiritual abuse, but divergence exists in the lack of integration across disciplinary boundaries. While trauma theorists document psychological outcomes, Black feminist and intersectional scholars focus on structural inequality, and critical religious studies emphasize theological distortions. Few studies synthesize these perspectives into a comprehensive framework, and the absence of culturally grounded, empirically tested interventions for communities like African American Muslims highlights both a methodological and conceptual gap.

This research addresses these gaps directly by applying Minority Stress Theory and Intersectionality Theory to the experiences of African American Muslims. MST explains how chronic social stressors such as racism, cultural erasure, and stigma exacerbate psychological distress, while Intersectionality illuminates how overlapping structures of oppression, racial, religious, and gendered, interact to produce unique forms of vulnerability. Extending these frameworks into the context of spiritual abuse advances theory by situating harm not only within individual trauma but also within broader structural, cultural, and theological systems.

Chapter 4:

Evolution of Spiritual Abuse Scholarship

The scholarly attention to spiritual abuse has evolved unevenly, moving from pastoral critique and sensationalized accounts of cultic harm toward more organized studies that examined religious harm through psychological, social, and moral perspectives. However, this progress has not been straightforward or complete.

Key conceptual breakthroughs, such as identifying clerical betrayal, institutional complicity, and the moral and knowledge-related aspects of spiritual harm, have helped the field move beyond personal stories. However, challenges remain in creating clear definitions, measurement methods, and fair representation. Chapter 4 follows this progress. It starts with the field's history in cult studies and church warnings, then explores ongoing debates over definitions that impact research and practice. It also reviews new classification methods for spiritual abuse, and concludes with an evaluation of progress and the remaining measurement issues that restrict both research, practical, and clinical applications.

4.1 Historical Roots

The modern scholarly engagement with spiritual harm traces its lineage through a sequence of intellectual moments. Early academic and popular attention often concentrated on high-visibility cases of charismatic leaders and destructive sects, instances in which extreme doctrinal control produced overt physical and collective harm. Analyses of Jonestown, the Branch Davidians, and other apocalyptic movements foregrounded the psychological mechanisms of coercion and group entrapment, framing spiritual harm as an extreme manifestation of manipulative leadership. These historical case studies highlighted how unchecked authority and closed epistemic systems can escalate into catastrophic outcomes, thereby legitimating the study of religious harm within psychology and the social sciences.

Parallel to these developments, pastoral and clinical commentators in the late 20th century began to articulate concerns about more diffuse forms of spiritual coercion within mainstream religious institutions. Johnson and VanVonderen's influential work introduced the term "spiritual abuse" to describe patterns of manipulation and control that did not fit neatly into earlier categories of cultic exploitation but nonetheless inflicted profound psychological and spiritual injury (Johnson & VanVonderen, 1991). Their pastoral orientation emphasized relational dynamics, how leaders' misuse of authority, doctrinal rigidity, and the spiritualization of control could destabilize congregants' sense of self and moral agency. Enroth and others extended these critiques into practical guidance for survivors, pastors, and counselors, offering early frameworks for recognition and recovery (Enroth, 1993; Enroth, 1994).

As the field matured, criminologists, sociologists, and psychologists began to incorporate theoretical models from coercive control research, betrayal trauma, and organizational studies. Freckelton (1998) and others argued that abuse within religious environments warrants the same legal and therapeutic scrutiny as other forms of institutional harm, especially since such institutions often shield offenders by claiming to uphold sacred authority.

Research on clergy sexual abuse in the Catholic Church further increased academic focus on institutional failures, revealing systemic patterns of cover-up and reputation protection that led to secondary victimization and long-term psychological effects. This body of work broadens the perspective from individual offenders to organizational systems, emphasizing how institutional responses, whether procedural, cultural, or theological, influence survivors' experiences.

The early development of spiritual abuse scholarship shows a shift from focusing on extreme to more common forms of harm. While initial research mainly looked at dramatic cult tragedies, later studies recognized that spiritual harm also occurs in everyday church life through doctrinal abuse, silence about misconduct, and the misuse of sacred language. This broader view has been important in bringing discussions about religious harm into mainstream mental health, pastoral care, and public policy, while also paving the way for later debates on definitions and categories.

4.2 Spiritual Abuse vs. Religious Abuse

One of the most persistent and significant debates in the field revolves around terminology and the scope of definitions. Different scholars draw varying boundaries between "spiritual abuse" and "religious abuse," affecting measurement, clinical diagnosis, and institutional accountability. Some early pastoral writings used these terms interchangeably, viewing spiritual abuse mainly as interpersonal manipulation under religious pretenses. Others suggested a clearer distinction: spiritual abuse as harm caused by doctrines and clerical dynamics at an individual or relational level, and religious abuse as institutional harm expressed through policies, hierarchies, or systemic practices.

This definitional difference matters because it affects both how prevalence is estimated and how interventions are designed. If spiritual abuse is narrowly defined as interpersonal doctrinal manipulation, then solutions may focus on pastoral supervision, survivor counseling, and setting interpersonal boundaries.

However, if religious abuse includes institutional practices, cover-ups, procedural neglect, and structural discrimination, then solutions require organizational reform, legal protections, and policies focused on transparency and accountability. The research shows the real-world effects of these definitional choices: studies on clergy sexual abuse often take an institutional view, noting betrayal and cover-ups, while research from pastoral counseling perspectives often addresses spiritual gaslighting, doctrinal coercion, and identity fragmentation on an interpersonal level.

The definitional debate also intersects with cultural and theological complexities. The meaning and experience of doctrinal authority vary widely across faith traditions and communities. A behavior interpreted as abusive in one context might be seen as legitimate pastoral care in another, complicating generalizations across traditions. Moreover, normative judgments about spiritual authority are themselves racialized and gendered: in racially stratified religious spaces, giving legitimacy to certain theological voices over others can serve as a form of epistemic injustice, thus blurring the lines between spiritual and religious abuse for marginalized groups. The literature therefore calls for careful operationalization that considers not only behaviors and outcomes but also the cultural logics that frame those behaviors as harmful or not.

Linguistically, the term "spiritual abuse" has gained popularity in both professional and general discussions, but its boundaries remain unclear. Some scholars criticize the term's vagueness and call for specific clinical criteria; others value the term's broadness because it allows survivors to describe harms that fall outside legal or medical categories. The field faces a crossroads: the need for clear definitions is urgent for scientific consistency and policy development, yet narrowing the meaning too much could invalidate survivors' complex experiences. Therefore, current research increasingly supports typological approaches that identify specific types of harm while acknowledging cultural differences.

4.3 Subtypes of Harm

To address definitional tensions, researchers have proposed taxonomies that categorize subtypes of spiritual and religious harm. One helpful taxonomy separates them into interpersonal, institutional, and doctrinal harms, each with different mechanisms and outcomes, though they often overlap in practice.

Interpersonal harm involves abuses within close relationships, such as between clergy and congregant, mentor and mentee, or among lay leaders, where power imbalances enable coercion. This category includes spiritual gaslighting, manipulation disguised as pastoral counseling, and coercive behaviors that take advantage of vulnerability (Knapp, 2021; Ward, 2011). Research on interpersonal spiritual abuse shows the loss of spiritual agency, persistent shame, and identity issues, with effects similar to betrayal trauma when the perpetrator is a trusted spiritual guide.

Institutional harm encompasses organizational practices and cultures that permit, conceal, or exacerbate abuse. This subtype is exemplified by cases in which institutions prioritize reputation, dismiss complaints, or create procedural barriers to accountability. Institutional harm includes systemic forms of neglect, such as failure to investigate allegations, collusion in victim-blaming, or governance structures that grant excessive discretion to unaccountable leaders. Institutional abuses produce secondary victimization and widespread mistrust in communal support systems, making recovery more difficult and often necessitating structural reform for meaningful redress.

Doctrinal harm involves religious teachings, scriptural interpretations, or narratives that, when misused, promote control, justify abuse, or place excessive moral burdens. Toxic theology often appears as perfectionist or retribution-based frameworks that view suffering as divine punishment or dissent as sin, leading to cognitive dissonance and internal shame. This type of harm is especially dangerous because it uses the sacred to justify coercion, making resistance feel morally wrong and complicating efforts to separate faith from harm.

Although these subtypes are conceptually different, they often work together. Doctrinal justifications can justify interpersonal coercion, and institutional silence can strengthen doctrinal authority by silencing alternative views. This research's qualitative data, for example, shows how doctrinal weaponization and institutional betrayal cause epistemic marginalization: survivors describe being delegitimized when they attempt to name abuse, with leaders framing their complaints as spiritual failings rather than institutional issues. This overlap emphasizes the need for interventions that address doctrinal education, relational boundaries, and institutional accountability all at once.

4.4 Measurement Efforts and Gaps in the Literature

As the field has matured conceptually, scholars have sought to operationalize spiritual and religious harm for empirical study. Measurement efforts have ranged from clinician-oriented trauma checklists to psychometrically validated scales designed to capture domains specific to spiritual abuse. The Spiritual Harm and Abuse Scale (SHAS), developed by Koch and Edstrom (2022), represents a notable advance: it operationalizes multiple dimensions of spiritual harm, authoritarian leadership, damaging God-image, institutional prioritization of reputation, and gender bias, through a 27-item instrument with demonstrated internal consistency. Similarly, measures of race-based traumatic stress, such as the Racial Trauma Scale (RTS) (Williams et al., 2022), provide tools for capturing the psychological consequences of racism that often intersect with religious dynamics in minority faith communities.

Despite these advances, important measurement gaps still exist. First, many existing instruments were created and normed on samples that do not adequately represent racially minoritized or religiously diverse populations. As a result, measures may fail to identify culturally specific forms of harm, such as how epistemic injustice is experienced by African American Muslims, or they may not distinguish between doctrinally based pastoral care and coercive theological manipulation. Second, the strong correlation often found between measures of spiritual abuse and racial trauma suggests a potential conceptual overlap that current measurement tools find difficult to differentiate; multicollinearity complicates statistical analysis of moderation or mediation in quantitative research. For example, in the dissertation's quantitative analysis, high correlations among SHAS, RTS, and psychological distress indicated these measures overlap significantly. This makes it challenging to interpret how they interact and suggests that the combined harms may intensify one another rather than simply add up.

A third challenge relates to the area of moral and epistemic injury. Traditional psychiatric tools focus on symptoms like anxiety, depression, and Post Traumatic Stress Disorder (PTSD), but may overlook specific outcomes such as a damaged God-image, loss of spiritual authority, or ongoing hermeneutical injustice. To capture these subtle outcomes, it is necessary to develop items and scales that address spiritual identity, trust in religious epistemic communities, and the ability to rebuild meaning after spiritual betrayal. Qualitative research remains essential for identifying these phenomena and guiding the development of quantitative measures.

Finally, methodological limitations affect much of the existing research: cross-sectional designs dominate, which restricts causal inference; small and convenience samples limit generalizability; and there is a notable lack of longitudinal, multilevel, and mixed-methods studies that can track patterns of harm and recovery over time. The dissertation's convergent mixed-methods approach, combining SHAS and RTS measurements with interpretative phenomenology, addresses some of these issues by allowing statistical analysis and narrative insights to inform one another. However, the broader field still needs larger, more diverse samples and longitudinal follow-ups to establish temporal sequences and intervention effects.

The study of spiritual abuse has advanced from dramatic case studies to a more sophisticated, multidisciplinary investigation that now identifies interpersonal, doctrinal, and institutional sources of harm. However, challenges such as definitional ambiguity, measurement gaps, and methodological limitations persist in the field. Overcoming these issues with culturally sensitive tools, multilevel research designs, and participatory methods will be crucial to translating academic insights into effective clinical practices, institutional reforms, and meaningful support for survivors. The following chapters build on this important foundation by combining empirical data and personal stories to explore paths toward healing and accountability in racially marginalized religious communities.

Chapter 5:

Racial Trauma and the Black Muslim Experience

Racial trauma is a widespread and harmful force that affects mental health in both obvious and subtle ways. For Black Muslims, experiences of anti-Black racism in society combine with feelings of exclusion within Muslim communities, creating a unique social and psychological situation that requires careful, culturally sensitive analysis. This chapter centers the Black Muslim experience to explain how racialized stressors function both conceptually and clinically. It highlights the specific forms of anti-Blackness encountered inside and outside Muslim spaces, traces intergenerational and neurobiological pathways through which racial trauma becomes embodied, and examines the complex aspects of Black Muslim identity, such as conversion, cultural heritage, and belonging, that influence risk and resilience.

Moving beyond simplistic views that treat race or religion separately, the chapter presents racial trauma as a multi-level phenomenon that interacts with spiritual life, institutional structures, and identity development, drawing from the dissertation's empirical findings and existing literature to highlight clinical and theoretical implications.

5.1 Racial Trauma: Conceptual and Clinical Features

Racial trauma refers to the cumulative psychological harm caused by experiences of racism, including sudden episodes of violence and ongoing exposure to discrimination, microaggressions, and systemic exclusion. Essentially, racial trauma is different from other types of posttraumatic stress because it originates from social sources: social systems, structures, and cultural narratives that devalue and dehumanize a group based on race.

Clinically, racial trauma presents as anxiety, hypervigilance, intrusion, avoidance, sleep issues, physical symptoms, and disruptions to identity and meaning. These symptom groups may overlap with PTSD measures but often include specific disturbances, racialized anticipatory fear, ongoing cognitive load from vigilance, and chronic grief related to collective loss that standard diagnostic criteria do not fully address.

The research synthesis highlights three interconnected clinical features of racial trauma. First, racial trauma is cumulative: individual incidents matter, but the frequent and widespread nature of racialized stressors builds an allostatic load that leads to long-term dysregulation. Second, racial trauma is relational: it is experienced through social networks and influenced by community resources, so the presence or lack of culturally appropriate support affects how symptoms develop.

Third, racial trauma is epistemic: experiences of racism are often dismissed, minimized, or misunderstood by dominant institutions, leading to testimonial silencing that worsens harm and discourages help-seeking (Brown & Kirschenbaum, 2021). These points highlight why clinicians working with Black Muslim clients need to assess both obvious traumatic experiences and subtle, identity-related stressors that damage trust, belonging, and meaning.

Importantly, racial trauma often operates in tandem with other identity-based stressors. For Black Muslims, Islamophobia in the broader society and intra-faith anti-Blackness are not additive afterthoughts but mutually constitutive processes that shape the content of traumatic experience. Where racialized encounters occur within sacred spaces or are minimized by religious authorities, the dissonance between spiritual expectations and lived experience can intensify moral and spiritual injury, producing a hybrid form of distress that straddles clinical and existential domains. The clinical consequence is that traditional trauma interventions that ignore the racialized and spiritual contours of suffering risk missing core drivers of distress and leaving survivors epistemically isolated.

5.2 Anti-Blackness Inside and Outside Muslim Spaces

Anti-Blackness influences Black Muslim life across various contexts, from encounters with law enforcement and employment discrimination to the daily microaggressions in schooling and healthcare. In mainstream U.S. society, anti-Black racial ideologies lead to higher exposure to policing, economic marginalization, and threats of violence, all of which cause traumatic stress for Black individuals. For Black Muslims, Islamophobic surveillance and racial profiling intensify these struggles, creating intersecting systems of stigma that mark both race and religion as vulnerable sites.

Yet anti-Blackness is not merely an external force. Within Muslim communities, heterogeneous, transnational, and stratified racial hierarchies often mirror those of the broader society. The dissertation documents patterns in which African American Muslims report feeling culturally marginalized, epistemically devalued, or delegated to subordinate positions within leadership structures.

These dynamics may include the preferential elevation of immigrant or majority-ethnic leaders, the dismissal of Black theological voices, or cultural gatekeeping that portrays African American religiosity as less authentic Islam. Such intra-faith biases cause specific harms: they limit access to authority, diminish credibility when safety concerns are voiced, and reinforce patterns of testimonial injustice similar to those in secular institutions. The real-life effects of intra-Muslim anti-Blackness are emotionally and spiritually damaging.

When Black congregants face racism within their places of worship, the experience often feels like a double betrayal—by society and by a community supposed to offer refuge. This double burden can worsen feelings of alienation and fracture spiritual trust. Survivors talk about being gaslit when raising concerns about racialized mistreatment, encountering minimization wrapped in calls for unity, or hearing that speaking out threatens communal cohesion. Institutional responses that prioritize reputation or harmony over equity and accountability effectively silence dissent and deepen epistemic wounds, creating an environment where racialized harms are repeatedly ignored rather than addressed.

Furthermore, the specific forms of anti-Blackness that occur within Muslim spaces are influenced by historical and geopolitical factors. The transnational nature of many Muslim communities means that racial hierarchies often mirror colonial or immigrant dynamics, privileging certain ethnicities, nationalities, or immigrant stories over African American heritage.

These dynamics complicate identity for Black Muslims whose religio-racial positioning does not neatly map onto dominant cultural scripts, forcing continuous negotiation of belonging and authenticity. Clinical work must therefore assess not only exposure to racist events but also how anti-Blackness is experienced within sacred contexts that are otherwise sources of meaning and belonging.

5.3 Intergenerational and Neurobiological Pathways

Racial trauma is not limited to immediate experiences; it is passed down across generations through socialization, storytelling, and increasingly documented biological processes (e.g., Epigenetics). Intergenerational transmission occurs through storytelling, parenting practices, communal memory, and cultural transmission of vigilance strategies. Families teach children how to recognize danger, navigate institutions, and interpret encounters with law enforcement or discrimination. These lessons influence development in ways that can be protective but also increase stress sensitivity. The qualitative narratives in the study show how older generations pass down histories of racial exclusion and religious marginalization, providing younger Black Muslims with both adaptive survival skills and a chronic sense of threat that can solidify into hypervigilant stress responses.

At the neurobiological level, chronic exposure to racial stressors contributes to allostatic load, causing wear and tear on physiological systems regulated by the hypothalamic-pituitary-adrenal axis, the autonomic nervous system, and inflammatory processes. Empirical research links ongoing discrimination to disrupted cortisol rhythms, increased cardiovascular risk, and elevated inflammatory markers, pathways that raise susceptibility to mood disorders, physical illness, and cognitive difficulties. For Black Muslims, who may face both religious and racial stressors simultaneously, the biological embedding of stress may be especially significant, leading to both immediate symptoms and long-term health disparities (Lewis et al., 2010; Williams et al., 2019).

Neurobiological models also help explain common clinical signs in racial trauma that do not always align with traditional PTSD patterns. Instead of isolated re-experiencing of specific traumatic events, many survivors display signs of chronic hyperarousal, sleep disturbances, and somatic symptoms, all indicating a persistent sense of threat. The mental effort from vigilance, constantly scanning for potential racialized threats, disrupts focus and memory, impairing daily functioning. Importantly, these biological responses are shaped by context: access to supportive community resources, validation from institutions, and opportunities for collective mourning and political action can lessen physiological stress responses and foster resilience.

Understanding intergenerational and neurobiological pathways highlights the importance of interventions that target both psychosocial and physical aspects. Trauma-informed care for Black Muslims should include somatic regulation, culturally grounded narrative work, and community-based strategies that facilitate collective processing of racial grief and resistance. These interventions must also address the political and structural causes of racial trauma; clinical treatment alone, without social action, risks turning issues into solely individual problems that are actually social in nature.

5.4 Black Muslim Identity

Black Muslim identity is diverse, shaped by a mix of conversion stories, longstanding African American Muslim traditions, and transnational influences that energize U.S. Muslim communities. Conversion stories, often seen as quests for dignity, spiritual freedom, or political awareness, are central to forming many Black Muslim identities. For many converts, Islam provides a theological and community framework that challenges white supremacy, highlights Black dignity, and connects religious practice with racial liberation stories. These conversion paths can be very empowering, offering new ways to find meaning and take social action.

Simultaneously, cultural heritage links many African American Muslims to extended histories of Black religious experience rooted in resilience, music, social protest, and prophetic traditions of justice. This heritage provides communal rituals, interpretive frameworks, and political languages that place religious life within struggles for racial equality. For many Black Muslims, the blending of Islamic and African American cultural memories creates hybrid practices, innovative theological syntheses, and community traditions that promote belonging and resilience amid external and internal marginalization.

Belonging, however, remains contested. Black Muslims often navigate tensions between asserting a unique African American Muslim identity and adapting to the cultural norms of transnational or immigrant Muslim majorities. Issues of authenticity, authority, and cultural compatibility can lead to intra-community conflicts. The dissertation's interviews show how some Black Muslims face conditional acceptance, being respected only if they meet certain expectations, while others face outright racial exclusion.

These dynamics influence both community engagement and help-seeking behavior; individuals who see their religious communities as safe and supportive are more likely to find resilience through faith, while those facing marginalization within their congregations often withdraw or look for alternative spiritual homes.

Identity formation also influences how people respond to spiritual abuse and racial trauma. Individuals with strong, integrated identities who can draw on conversion stories and cultural memory to interpret harm within larger stories of resistance may be better able to externalize blame and gather social support. Conversely, those whose identities are fractured by racial rejection or doctrinal invalidation face higher risks of internalized shame and epistemic confusion.

Therefore, interventions that enhance identity coherence through communal recognition, theological reclamation, and culturally sensitive therapeutic practices can serve as protective measures. The literature indicates that approaches focusing on narrative repair, collective ritual, and community accountability effectively restore a sense of belonging and reduce the ongoing impacts of racial and spiritual trauma.

In sum, racial trauma for Black Muslims must be recognized as a multi-dimensional phenomenon: it results from societal anti-Blackness, influenced by intra-faith racial hierarchies, experienced through intergenerational and neurobiological processes, and shaped by complex identity formations focused on conversion and cultural heritage. Clinicians, researchers, and community leaders aware of these dynamics can better customize interventions that respect both spiritual resources and specific vulnerabilities of Black Muslim communities, addressing trauma in ways that are culturally relevant, politically aware, and institutionally responsible.

Part III

Empirical Findings (Study-Based Chapters)

Chapter 6:

Methods

Part III delivers the core empirical analysis of this publication: a convergent mixed-methods study on how spiritual harms and racial trauma combine to influence psychological distress among African American Muslims. Chapter 6 explains the study's methodological reasoning and procedures, framing these choices within the study's commitments to Minority Stress Theory and Intersectionality.

6.1 Sampling, Recruitment, and Participant Demographics

Sampling combined purposive and snowball methods to identify adults who self-identify as African American (or Black/African diasporic) and Muslim, with relevant experience in mosque or community settings. Purposive sampling ensured participants met specific experience criteria (i.e., reported spiritual harm and racialized stress), while snowball referral helped reach less-visible survivors, aligning with best practices for studying stigmatized, hard-to-reach populations. The sampling focused on metropolitan areas with established African American Muslim networks on the East Coast of the United States.

Recruitment combined community partnership outreach (flyers, presentations, organizational listservs) with targeted social media advertising and private group invitations. Partnerships with women-led community organizations and local Muslim mental health practitioners added credibility and supported trauma-informed referral pathways. All outreach stressed voluntary participation, confidentiality, trauma-informed safeguards, and access to culturally competent referrals. Contact information for follow-up interviews was collected separately from anonymous surveys to maintain respondent anonymity.

The study planned and achieved sample sizes that reflected different priorities for the quantitative and qualitative strands. For the quantitative part, a planned sample size of 150 to 200 was set to support complex data analysis and interaction tests, but the final sample used for the main regressions was 127, due to recruitment limits and data quality checks. For the qualitative strand, an Interpretative Phenomenological Analysis–appropriate purposive subsample of 5 participants was targeted, and 5 in-depth interviews were conducted and analyzed, consistent with IPA guidance that values depth and idiographic richness over large samples.

The quantitative sample (n = 127) included adults aged 19 to 68, with an average age in the mid-30s. It consisted of a mix of native-born and converted individuals, with most respondents identifying as converts, which aligns with national trends. Educational levels ranged from high school to graduate degrees, and relationship statuses included single, married, separated, and divorced. The embedded qualitative subsample (n = 5) was intentionally selected from survey respondents who reported both SHAS and RTS experiences and volunteered for interviews. This purposive sampling aimed to include diversity in congregational roles and help-seeking histories to enhance analytical insights.

The purposive/snowball method sacrifices broad statistical accuracy to better align with theory and real-life experience. This method was chosen deliberately because of the focus on overlapping social factors and the need to include people with specific personal experiences. Efforts to expand outreach via social media and multiple community partners, along with documentation of sampling biases such as self-selection and network clustering, were undertaken and reported to enable readers to interpret the findings cautiously.

6.2 Instruments

Instrument selection focused on conceptual resonance with the constructs previously outlined and ensured psychometric rigor. The SHAS measured spiritually framed harms and institutional dynamics; the RTS assessed race-based traumatic stress outcomes; and the psychological-distress index gauged symptom severity across depression, anxiety, and trauma-related areas. Instruments were utilized in their validated versions where available, and cognitive checks confirmed that item wording aligned with participants' religious language.

The conceptual domain and development of the Spiritual Harms and Abuse Scale (SHAS) assess doctrinal weaponization, spiritual gaslighting, institutional silencing, gendered bias, and related constructs that correspond to mechanisms previously discussed (e.g., doctrinal manipulation, institutional betrayal). The study employed the 27-item SHAS (Appendix B), scored according to the original validation procedures (item means and subscale aggregation). Evidence from the current test includes: strong reliability, with a consistency score of .93 ($\alpha = .93$); a factor structure that matches the original study; and a meaningful link between high SHAS scores and key themes. Questions were reviewed through interviews with community advisors to improve religious wording and cultural details.

The conceptual domain and development of the Racial Trauma Scale (RTS) evaluate multidimensional race-based traumatic stress, including affective distress, hypervigilance or arousal, intrusive thoughts, avoidance, and somatic or behavioral reactions. The 30-item RTS used in this study (see Appendix C) operationalizes racial trauma as a chronic, identity-based stressor aligned with Minority Stress concepts. Psychometric data from this sample show internal consistency with $\alpha = .91$ and strong bivariate links to the psychological-distress index, supported by interview narratives that describe race as an amplifier of spiritual harms.

Psychological distress was measured as a combined result, and its link to spiritual abuse and racial trauma was studied using simple and multiple statistical tests. The results confirmed the patterns shown in the attachment, with the combined psychological distress score showing strong reliability in the group studied ($\alpha \approx .92$). These statistical methods supported the idea that spiritually abusive experiences and race-related trauma are connected to psychological distress.

Before fielding, instruments underwent cultural and theological validity checks with a small panel of community advisors representing diversity in age, nativity, and congregational roles. Feedback led to minor wording adjustments (e.g., substituting "spiritual harm" language that matched participants' idioms) and to clarifications of confidentiality language regarding reporting to mosque authorities. These steps increased face validity and reduced hermeneutic mismatch between the researcher's language and the participant's conceptual repertoires.

6.3 Trustworthiness/Validity and Reliability of the Data

To ensure that the study's findings rest on sound evidence, I implemented and documented procedures to assess and protect the trustworthiness, validity, and reliability of both the quantitative and qualitative data. The following describes those procedures and the key outcomes relevant to data integrity, measurement quality, and interpretive credibility. Detailed numeric diagnostics and time-stamped audit records are reported with the Results to preserve transparency and reproducibility.

Quantitative Strand

The numerical results indicate that the measurements are highly reliable and the data is precise. The main scales were consistent: the SHAS had a reliability of .93, the RTS .91, and the combined psychological-distress index .92. The scale scores, which are averages of the items, performed as expected, with higher scores indicating greater exposure or more severe symptoms. Item content clearly aligned with key concepts emphasized in the study, such as doctrinal weaponization, testimonial de-legitimation, and somatic manifestations. Missing data within scales was minimal and did not significantly affect scale distributions or conclusions. Distribution measures (skewness, kurtosis) and residual checks showed no violations of model assumptions that could impact interpretation. Checks for overlapping information between variables remained within acceptable limits for the analysis. Tests demonstrated consistent estimates and effect patterns, confirming the reliability of the numerical results in subsequent models.

Qualitative Strand

The qualitative findings support credibility, transferability, dependability, and confirmability. Credibility is supported by participants' own clarifications and brief elaborations that reinforce core meanings, and by verbatim exemplar quotations that consistently anchor Personal Experiential Themes (PETs) and Group Experiential Themes (GETs), allowing readers to follow how interpretations emerge from the data. Transferability was strengthened by detailed, contextual descriptions of participants' circumstances and community settings, presented alongside the themes, providing readers with the information they need to evaluate how the findings might be applicable in other contexts. Dependability is demonstrated through consistent coding and theme boundaries, high inter-coder agreement, and peer review, which highlight the stability of the analytic results and are supported by documented reflections tracking how interpretations evolved over time. Confirmability was shown through transparent audit records and reflexive notes documenting analytic decisions and researcher perspectives, along with clear links between each thematic claim and participant language, enabling independent assessment of the evidence. Attention to participant well-being during data collection also appears to have fostered honest disclosures, strengthening the authenticity of the accounts shared here.

Cross-Strand Integration and Transparency

Integration safeguards were deployed to align and interrogate findings across strands (see Appendix D). Psychometric results, such as item-level performance or unexpected distributional features, were compared with qualitative content to identify areas where instruments captured or failed to capture culturally specific expressions of harm. Where quantitative diagnostics suggested departures from expected scale behavior, the qualitative material was examined to determine whether the departures reflected meaningful cultural or contextual variance. Discrepancies between numeric patterns and narrative accounts were recorded and subjected to additional analytic scrutiny.

All decisions affecting interpretation, scale choice, handling missing data, coding options, and theme consolidation were recorded in time-stamped logs to ensure traceability from raw data to final conclusions. Overall, the study used multiple, complementary methods to evaluate and improve the reliability and validity of quantitative measures and to maintain credibility, dependability, and confirmability in qualitative analysis. The outcomes of these methods are included with the Results, giving readers and reviewers direct access to diagnostic values, example quotations, and the documented analytic process.

6.4 Evaluation of Findings

Comparison of Results to the Literature

This section places the study's empirical results within the literature summarized in Part II above, highlighting points of agreement and disagreement while offering plausible explanations for any differences from previous research. The citations below refer to the key studies and theoretical frameworks reviewed earlier and are used to support comparisons between this study's quantitative and qualitative findings and existing knowledge about spiritual abuse, racial trauma, and their mental health consequences.

Convergence with Prior Evidence

The study's quantitative finding that higher levels of reported spiritual abuse (SHAS scores) were strongly linked to increased psychological distress aligns with a growing body of research connecting the misuse of religious authority to lasting mental health issues. Empirical studies and clinical reviews have shown links between spiritually abusive behaviors (e.g., authoritarian control, shaming, doctrinal weaponization) and symptoms such as anxiety, depression, identity disruption, and complicated grief (Awaad & Riaz, 2022; Rhee, 2024).

The current internal-consistency results (high alpha values for the SHAS) and supporting qualitative themes, such as participant narratives describing the erosion of self-worth, chronic hypervigilance, and a sense of ruptured belonging within religious communities, align with previous accounts and extend them specifically to African American Muslim adults. This convergence suggests that spiritual abuse functions through psychosocial mechanisms (such as authority-based coercion and testimonial silencing) that are not limited to specific faith traditions and that produce identifiable symptom patterns across different affected populations.

Alignment with Literature

Quantitatively, the strong link observed between racial trauma scores (RTS) and psychological distress in this sample reflects extensive evidence that race-based traumatic stress significantly contributes to anxiety, depression, somatic symptoms, and posttraumatic stress–like responses. Qualitative accounts in this study, which described cumulative exposures to interpersonal discrimination, institutional marginalization, and historical narratives of exclusion, highlight themes that prior research identifies as central to racial trauma: chronic threat perception, anticipatory stress, and loss of cultural safety. Therefore, both aspects of this study support the literature's portrayal of racial trauma as a powerful factor in psychological suffering among racially minoritized groups.

Intersectional and Compounding Effects

Part I identified a conceptual and empirical gap regarding how spiritual abuse and racial trauma co-occur and collectively impact mental health, especially within Muslim communities of color. The present study's combined findings directly address this gap. Quantitative moderation analysis and qualitative theme integration showed that racial trauma and spiritual abuse often coexist and can have additive or synergistic effects on distress.

This pattern aligns with intersectionality-informed arguments in the literature, which argue that overlapping systems of oppression, racial marginalization, and religiously sanctioned authority abuses create unique, complex harms not fully captured by studies examining each domain separately. By documenting both statistical connections and narrative descriptions of how racialized forms of exclusion influence the experience and impact of spiritual abuse (such as racialized epistemic invalidation within congregational settings), the study builds on previous calls for intersectional measurement and theory development.

Points of Divergence

While many findings align with previous research, some differences emerged. First, certain aspects of spiritual abuse that are well-known in broader literature, such as clearly coercive financial exploitation, were less frequently reported or less strongly associated with distress in this sample than doctrinal control and testimonial silencing. This difference could result from community-specific patterns of abuse, sampling variations (since this study focused on community insiders, who may experience different patterns), or measurement details in which existing tools emphasize forms of abuse more common in other faith settings (Rhee, 2024).

The qualitative data suggest that, within the studied community, more subtle forms of knowledge (epistemic) exclusion and spiritual gatekeeping carried disproportionate psychosocial weight, emphasizing the need for culturally sensitive approaches. Additionally, some resilience and meaning-making patterns described in the literature, such as collective healing through organized religious support, appeared in participant narratives but did not consistently lessen measured distress. Prior research has observed religion's mixed role as both a potential source of harm and a coping strategy.

The current findings suggest that when religious institutions themselves are the source of abuse or racialized exclusion, traditional faith-based coping resources may be weakened; this detail helps explain why qualitative evidence of community support did not always lead to lower quantitative distress scores. Differences in institutional trust and access to culturally matching mental-health resources likely influence whether faith communities serve mainly as protective or harmful environments.

6.5 Analytic Procedures and Integration

Integration followed the convergent mixed methods approach outlined by Creswell and Plano Clark (2017). The process adhered to the written Integration Protocol in Appendix D. Quantitative and qualitative analyses were conducted independently and simultaneously. Integration took place during the interpretation phase. This method allowed each strand's strengths to contribute to a cohesive understanding. Joint displays linked qualitative themes to individual quantitative scores for consenting participants. These matrices facilitated case-by-case comparisons and helped identify where findings aligned or differed. The joint displays were based on procedures recommended by Fettcrs et al. (2013), enabling a clear, auditable comparison between lived experiences and numerical data.

Decision rules guided the classification of integrated claims. Claims were labeled Strong when statistical significance aligned with a clear qualitative mechanism. Claims were labeled "tentative" when one strand offered robust support, and the other offered partial or contextual support. Claims were labeled Divergent when the strands exhibited productive dissonance requiring further theoretical development.

Triangulation used three matching approaches. Convergence increased trust in cause-and-effect links related to minority stress theory. Complementarity used detailed methods to explain why statistical connections appeared. Divergence showed limitations in measurements and in situations that need further study. This ongoing exchange between data and stories helped create combined interpretations. The integration framework was based on principles outlined by Bauer et al. (2021).

Strong connections among the main variables made it hard to test their interactions. Analysts checked for overlapping information and tried different model setups. They also used additional tests, such as adjustments for residual effects and specialized regression methods. Unstable results were treated carefully. Stories and descriptions were used to identify shared patterns as possible signs of real combined trauma rather than mere measurement errors. These analytic safeguards were informed by recent methodological work (Chen et al., 2024).

Chapter 7:

Results and Patterns of Association

This chapter presents the main quantitative findings and the related interview material that bring the numbers to life. The survey included 127 African American Muslim adults who completed measures of spiritual harm, racial trauma, and psychological distress. The measurement scales showed strong internal consistency and large associations among the three constructs. Below, I present each research question with a brief statement of the quantitative results, followed by qualitative interview excerpts that illustrate how survivors experienced these harms.

Research Question 1: What is the relationship between spiritual abuse and psychological distress?

Quantitatively, spiritual abuse and psychological distress were closely linked. The Spiritual Harm and Abuse Scale aligned well with the distress measure, and the analysis showed it accounted for a significant portion of the distress. The model passed basic tests, and the scale was highly consistent within this group. However, the participants' interviews added a human dimension to that connection. Participants described spiritual environments that felt controlling, shaming, and unsafe. One woman said, "They would tell me I was not submissive enough and that my doubts were a sin. I started to think that I must be broken." Another female participant described repeated pressure from the masjid and home that wore down her self-esteem: "I wanted to be a good woman and felt pressure to conform. I kept asking myself if I was the problem, if I just wasn't patient enough." A young man who had been told he was morally defective said, "They made me feel like I had no right to question anything. I just swallowed it and got smaller."

Several participants linked these spiritual harms to clear psychological symptoms. "I felt jaded," one woman reported. "I became more self-aware, and then I couldn't stop blaming myself." Another explained how isolation followed: "I have just become so secluded in an effort to protect myself. What has developed from that is a sense of social anxiety." A clinical diagnosis was not uncommon. "I was diagnosed with depression," a participant said. "My anxiety worsened." The most heartbreaking account came from Bala (her pseudonym). She described being driven to a suicide attempt after prolonged spiritual and relationship pressures: "I was mentally finished with life. I went into the room, and I put the letter out for my daughters, and I took more pills." Her words highlight the human toll behind the statistical findings, emphasizing its real and urgent impact.

Participants also described specific spiritual mechanisms that caused harm. "It wasn't Allah, it was patriarchal interpretation," one woman said. "They used scripture to police my body and my choices." Another recalled the policing of dress and behavior: "Other women policed my buttons. They told me to wear black. It was like they cared more about appearances than about my suffering." Those kinds of experiences made it hard to maintain religious practice. "I stopped praying the way I used to. I felt like I was performing for them rather than connecting to God," a participant explained.

For survivors of spiritual abuse, the key point is that such abuse can cause real and lasting psychological distress. The data show how strong this connection is, and the interviews illustrate what that distress looks like in everyday life. If you notice these patterns in your own experience, understand that your distress is not an overreaction. It's a response to repeated harm. Practical steps that helped participants included finding people who listened, learning more about theology in ways that felt freeing, and seeking clinical support that respects your religious background. One participant summed up the way forward by saying, "Access to information helped me reframe. Finding someone who would just listen saved me."

Research Question 2: What is the relationship between racial trauma and psychological distress?

Quantitatively, racial trauma was very strongly associated with psychological distress. The Racial Trauma Scale correlated highly with the distress composite and showed high internal consistency. The association was among the strongest observed in the study. Interview accounts show how racial dynamics inside and outside religious spaces deepened distress. "They treated me like because I am Black, I could not know Islam," Aneesah said. "Whether it be not being greeted, or the salaams not being returned, you are being treated as if because you are Black, you can't know about Islam." Another participant described doubt cast on his authority: "He figured that you, as an African American, were not as qualified to be telling these young guys about Islam." These experiences left these participants feeling unseen and demeaned.

Participants identified specific forms of epistemic exclusion that intensified harm. "If you spoke up in a meeting, they would speak over you or reframe what you said as if you didn't know your place," Cana said. "They would make your contribution invisible." A woman who sought help after experiencing abuse felt racialized delegitimization in the response she received: "When I sought help, community leaders prioritized preserving the marriage over protecting my safety. It felt like my race made me disposable in that community," Bala said.

Those experiences led to emotional and psychological effects. One participant recalled, "I felt anger, but I also felt exhausted and ashamed for feeling angry." Another described the gradual buildup of stress: "Every time I tried to belong, something smaller and smaller chipped away at me. The constant reminders that I am not quite welcome wore me down."

Survivors described practical responses that provided relief. One person found comfort in Black Muslim study groups that affirmed both faith and racial identity. "Being with other Black Muslims saved my faith," she said. Others highlighted the importance of therapists who understand racial trauma. "Talking to someone who could identify the racial issues made a big difference," a participant said. When institutions dismissed complaints, participants advised documenting incidents and finding allies who would advocate openly.

Research Question 3: Does racial trauma change how spiritual abuse relates to psychological distress?

The quantitative moderation test did not produce a clear result. The interaction between racial trauma and spiritual abuse was unstable in statistical models, and the confidence interval included zero. Diagnostics showed very high shared variance among spiritual harm, racial trauma, and distress that inflated standard errors and made interaction terms unreliable. For that reason, the numeric report focuses on the main effects rather than on moderation.

Nevertheless, the qualitative participant interviews explain why the interaction test appeared unstable. Survivors did not experience spiritual abuse and racial trauma as separate issues; instead, they described harms that overlapped and merged. "They reframed my interventions as evidence of personal instability," Cana explained. "They called me angry, and then they dismissed my concerns." Daliah connected marital coercion to a larger pattern of institutional minimization: "When I sought help, community leaders prioritized preserving the marriage over protecting my safety." Institutional betrayal was a recurring theme. "They gave priority to protecting reputations instead of hearing me," one participant said. "I kept being told to slow down, stop talking, be patient."

These narratives reveal intersectional suffering. A woman might be silenced with spiritual rhetoric and then dismissed through racial stereotypes. "They called me the angry Black woman when I tried to get help," a participant said. "Then they would reframe what I said and make it my fault." Another described how the combined effect felt multiplicative rather than additive: "It was not just one thing. It was the religion stuff and the race stuff and the way the institution covered for leaders. It all mixed together, and I could not breathe."

From a survivor perspective, responses should focus on overlaps rather than distinctions. Support that isolates spiritual harm will overlook how racial exclusion influences both exposure to harm and access to redress. Participants suggested integrated advocacy that addresses both spiritual injury and racial invalidation. One participant said, "You cannot fix the spiritual harm without fixing the way race plays out in the community. They protect leaders and ignore Black people at the same time."

The quantitative results show strong links between spiritual harm, racial trauma, and psychological distress. The qualitative quotes add depth to these links and illustrate how the harms feel and develop. Simultaneously, the high overlap among these areas makes it hard to clearly separate cause and effect.

Numbers can't capture timing, lived experience, or the ongoing processes that interviews reveal. For survivors, the key messages are twofold. First, the harm is real and meaningful. Bala's story of a suicide attempt, along with multiple reports of depression and anxiety, demonstrates that spiritual and racial wounds deeply affect mental health. Second, healing and justice require approaches that recognize both spiritual injury and racial exclusion. Participants found support from listening allies, faith communities that respect racial identity, clinicians who understand religion and race, and advocacy that documents the combined harms. As one participant said, "We need people who will see all of who we are and stand with us when we say we are hurt."

Research Question 4: How African American Muslims interpret and give meaning to their lived experiences of spiritual abuse and racial trauma within their religious communities.

This question was explored only qualitatively through the semi-structured interviews. The survey data helped contextualize the interviews, but did not address meaning-making questions. What follows highlights shared patterns that emerged across participants, using many of their own words so readers can see how survivors make sense of what happened to them and how they responded.

Participants mostly described spiritual abuse as a relational injury that was both epistemic and doctrinal. They shared experiences of being silenced, having their knowledge dismissed, and seeing scripture or religious language used to shame and coerce. Abdul recalled others assuming that "you, as an African American, were not as qualified to be telling these young guys about Islam." Aneesah described daily, small rejections that signaled larger exclusion: "Whether it be not being greeted, or the salaams not being returned…you're being treated as if because you are Black you can't know about Islam." Deliah explained how doctrine was weaponized against her objections: "They'd say I was being 'divisive' or 'rebellious' whenever I pointed out how rules were being enforced differently." Those experiences led many to believe that the problem was not their faith but the people and practices surrounding it. One participant plainly stated, "Islam is the truth, but the people are not following Islam."

These relational dynamics affected individuals' identities and bodies equally. Testimonial invalidation and doctrinal pressure fostered self-doubt, shame, and hypervigilance that often fractured religious identity. Aneesah described withdrawing from others to protect herself and then noticing the psychological toll: "I have just become so secluded in an effort of protecting myself … I've closed myself off … social anxiety." Bala experienced somatic and mental crises after repeated pressures: "I went to the hospital due to uncontrolled blood pressure … I was mentally finished with life..." For many participants, the inner question became whether their faith was the source of harm or if spiritual language had been misused. One woman explained the distinction this way: "It wasn't Allah, it was patriarchal interpretation."

The context usually shaped the harms. Leadership failures and anti-Black norms turned interpersonal injury into institutional betrayal. When survivors sought help, they often encountered protection of reputation rather than protection of people. Cana said leaders "gave priority to protecting reputations instead of hearing me. I kept being told to slow down, ... be patient." Cana described deliberate marginalization by prominent leaders: "very prominent imams intentionally created Fitnah … pushing us … to the side so that our voices weren't heard." These patterns left participants feeling that institutions were not only blind to their suffering but also actively complicit in keeping harmful dynamics in place.

Racial dynamics heightened spiritual harm and influenced perceptions of who was believed. Participants described the emotional toll of being treated as a suspect or disposable. Aneesah recalled, "You were made to feel that unless you dressed in black, you were being disobedient or you were not being pleasing to Allah." Cana admitted that when they called her "the angry Black woman," this label was then "...used to dismiss" her. When testimony is dismissed, harm increases. Cana explained how speaking up often led to being talked over and misrepresented: "If you spoke up in a meeting, they would speak over you or reframe what you said as if you didn't know your place." Bala reflected on how racialized treatment influenced help-seeking: "It felt like my race made me disposable in that community."

The outcomes were clear and specific. Participants connected the combined harms to withdrawing from community life, losing a sense of belonging, and making practical changes in how they participated. Aneesah described spiritual disruption and periods of numbness: "I struggle with periods of not praying ... sometimes I would just be in bed for days." Cana talked about redirecting her resources and stepping back from institutional life: "I don't say I'm of this community anymore. I put my money and my spending; my charitable giving goes to individual institutions, not to masjids." Another participant summarized the erosion of trust by saying, "They gave priority to protecting reputations instead of hearing me," which made further participation feel unsafe.

Despite this harm, participants actively worked to reclaim their agency and rebuild meaning. Reclamation took many forms. Daliah pursued religious study to regain authority and protect others: "I wanted to learn my religion so I could come back and teach the sisters, because I didn't want any sisters to go through what I experienced." Cana redirected financial support as a boundary and a form of protest: "I put my charitable giving to individual institutions, not to masjids." Others formed peer networks or sought therapists who understood both faith and race. One participant described the relief of finding a space that honored both identities by saying, "Being with other Black Muslims saved my faith." Another explained how learning more about theology helped her reframe painful experiences: "Access to information helped me reframe. Finding someone who would just listen saved me."

From a survivor-focused perspective, these meanings point to practical priorities for healing and reform. Survivors taught that addressing spiritual abuse requires attention to the ways race shapes credibility and access. One participant advised that you cannot repair spiritual harm without addressing racial dynamics: "You cannot fix the spiritual harm without fixing the way race plays out in the community. They protect leaders and ignore Black people at the same time." Survivors recommended transparent complaint pathways, leadership accountability, redistribution of interpretive authority, and trauma-informed clinical care that preserves spiritual resources while addressing institutional harms. They urged institutions to listen without defaulting to the preservation of reputation and to create clear, safe ways for marginalized voices to be heard.

In short, participants viewed their experiences as complex and interconnected. Spiritual abuse was rarely solely about doctrine; it encompassed relationships, bodies, institutions, and social meaning. Racialized exclusion intensified spiritual harm and made recovery more challenging. However, survivors also shared specific acts of resistance and reclamation that helped them regain faith and identity. Their stories demonstrate both how harm is inflicted and how it can be healed. As one participant said, "We need people who will see all of who we are and stand with us when we say we are hurt."

Chapter 8:

Integrative Analysis

Chapter 8 weaves together numbers and stories to argue that spiritual abuse and racial trauma in African American Muslim contexts are not separate problems that simply add up. They are intertwined processes shaped by congregational practices and leadership choices. The survey showed very large associations among spiritually abusive experiences, race-based traumatic stress, and psychological distress. The interviews showed how ordinary interactions in religious settings translate those social inequalities into felt, embodied suffering. When the statistical patterns and the personal accounts are read together, a clearer picture emerges. The two strands amplify one another and point toward a single, compound phenomenon that demands integrated responses.

The quantitative findings were impressive in their consistency. Measures of spiritual harm and racial trauma both showed strong correlations with measures of distress. These relationships remained consistent across various checks and analytical approaches. These numbers indicate that the psychosocial burden in this sample is significant. At the same time, the high overlap between the measures suggests that the dataset cannot clearly distinguish what is uniquely spiritual harm from what is specifically racial trauma. Instead of viewing this ambiguity as a flaw, the interviews help explain why it occurs. Participants described experiences where spiritual rhetoric erased their testimony and racialized attitudes determined whose suffering was acknowledged. The narratives clarify the statistical overlap because they demonstrate the same event being both spiritual abuse and racialized invalidation simultaneously.

There are points where the strands diverge and others where both stay quiet. The survey provides scale scores and correlations, but cannot reveal details about timing, personal significance, or the step-by-step processes that happen week by week. The interviews add depth to these processes, but we cannot determine how representative each pattern is of larger groups. Together, they reveal what the numbers and stories alone cannot. The combined account, therefore, draws on both types of evidence to make careful claims about mechanisms and outcomes.

Three institutional pathways most clearly turn congregational practices into layered harm. First, doctrinal weaponization occurs when religious language is used selectively to shame, silence, or control specific members. Participants described the Quran and Sunnah traditions as tools for enforcing obedience and dismissing dissent. Second, epistemic exclusion happens when racialized assumptions devalue the knowledge and testimony of Black congregants. This exclusion damages credibility and shifts complaints away from genuine protection. Third, reputational protection influences institutional responses that prioritize the community's or leaders' reputation over the safety of those reporting harm. This protection often perpetuates neglect and re-traumatization. Each pathway interacts with the others. Shaming doctrinal language can be strengthened by racialized disbelief and an institutional tendency to protect reputation. Together, these form a mechanism by which congregational life causes layered psychospiritual injury.

Building on these pathways, a working multilevel model locates harm across nested domains. At the individual level, people experience shame, identity fracture, somatic symptoms, and emotional numbing. At the interpersonal level, relationships and power dynamics determine who can speak and who will be heard. At the institutional level, leadership choices, complaint processes, and norms of reputation management shape whether harm is acknowledged or denied. Structural forces of racism and gendered authority flow through each layer and shape patterns of exposure and redress. This model treats spiritual abuse and racial trauma as co-occurring forces that are mutually constitutive rather than separable causes.

The most urgent implications are both practical and moral. When spiritual abuse and racial trauma intersect, the psychological and social consequences are profound. People lose trust, withdraw from community life, and may even face clinical crises. The study shows that meaningful responses must be intersectional. Reforms that focus only on doctrine without addressing racial credibility issues, or that address only race without reforming complaint processes, will overlook the complex nature of the harm. Survivors need trauma-informed care that acknowledges religious meaning and racial identity. Institutions require transparent accountability and the redistribution of interpretive authority so no one has to choose between faith and safety. The evidence presented in this chapter emphasizes the need for both healing and institutional change to converge. Viewing these harms as interconnected parts of a single problem leads to more honest diagnoses and more effective solutions.

8.1 The Role of Vulnerability

Vulnerability lies at the heart of how harm happens in religious communities. Both participants in this study and a wide range of scholarship agree on this point. Vulnerability is not a sign of personal weakness; it is a natural human trait that encourages connection, dependence, and trust (Langberg, 2020). When these conditions are valued, vulnerability can enrich spiritual growth and foster genuine empathy. However, in the absence of ethical responsibility, vulnerability becomes a gateway for manipulation, control, and abuse. This fundamental dynamic helps explain why spiritual abuse and racial trauma often combine to create a double injury for African American Muslims.

Research has described vulnerability in complementary ways that illuminate what happens to marginalized people inside congregations (Gray et al., 2021; Sanchini et al., 2022). Some scholars speak of specific vulnerabilities that arise from age, health, disability, or life circumstance. Children, elders, and people with illnesses or disabilities often rely on others for care and instruction. In religious settings that rely on moral authority or hierarchical power, that reliance can be exploited. Other scholars describe anthropological vulnerability (Platovnjak, 2024) as the universal human condition of dependence and relational need. This second sense highlights that everyone is exposed, even when not obviously disadvantaged. When leaders treat that universal dependence as a lever for control rather than a responsibility to protect, the results are existential.

The lived consequences for vulnerable and marginalized people are severe. Testimony is often the first to be lost. When someone discusses harm and is met with dismissal, disbelief, or reframing, their right to describe their own experience is taken away. That loss of credibility affects both psychological and social aspects. It becomes harder to find meaningful help. It also damages trust in leaders, peers, and the moral language that once provided a sense of belonging. Survivors describe this as more than just hurtful treatment. Demasure (2022) identifies the loss of self as one of the most damaging results of spiritual abuse, where victims face a deep erosion of identity, agency, and meaning. Survivors describe themselves as "no longer a person" or "a shadow of myself," reflecting not only psychological injury but also the destruction of their ability to exist as autonomous, relational beings.

Marginalization inside congregations often compounds the harms that exist outside them. Said differently, to be treated hurtfully in the mosque is worse than being ill-treated on the outside. Racialized assumptions can make Black congregants less likely to be believed when they name abuse or to be seen as authorities in religious life. Gendered expectations can narrow the space in which women speak and act. Disability, lack of religious knowledge, or the Arabic language is often used to alter the balance of power in ways that concentrate risk on certain bodies and voices.

In practice, this means that when someone from a marginalized group seeks help, the institutional response is more likely to focus on protecting reputation, maintaining leadership, or dismissing the complaint. This pattern turns an individual injury into institutional betrayal. Vulnerable people are then punished twice: they endure the original harm and also suffer within a system that refuses to recognize their pain as deserving of care.

Psychological effects follow predictable patterns. Shame and self-doubt take hold when sacred language is weaponized. A spiritual framework that once provided meaning becomes a source of contradiction and moral confusion. Anxiety rises when people realize that telling the truth about their experience won't offer protection. For many, withdrawal becomes a survival strategy. Stepping back from community life reduces immediate exposure but also cuts off access to social support and culturally grounded resources. While this withdrawal may seem like a safety move, over time it leads to loneliness and secondary harms.

Bodies also register this layered injury. As Van der Kolk (2014) said, the body keeps score. Chronic stress from living in invalidating environments manifests as sleep problems, persistent pain, increased blood pressure, and other somatic symptoms. The combination of racial stress and spiritual betrayal creates a physiological burden that clinical settings must take seriously. Without integrated care that recognizes how meaning and the body are intertwined, survivors can be left in clinics that treat only one domain of suffering while the other continues to weaken resilience.

The social and moral consequences are equally real. When people lose trust in community networks and institutions, they also lose access to mutual aid systems, informal caregiving, and the cultural rituals that foster a sense of belonging. Young people who see elders or leaders dismiss marginalized voices learn where power really lies and whose suffering is valued. Families can break apart as survivors struggle to find support. The overall effect is a diminished community ability to respond to harm when it happens, and a shift towards norms that protect reputation over people's well-being.

Scholars and survivors highlight the processes that make these outcomes more likely. When vulnerability is seen as weakness instead of a call to care, leaders may misuse doctrine, silence dissent, and prioritize institutional stability over healing. When racialized credibility gaps exist, the burden of proof falls more heavily on marginalized complainants. When institutional complaint channels are unclear or controlled by those concerned about their reputation, survivors learn that speaking out will cost them and rarely lead to consequences for the guilty parties. These factors do not work separately; they are connected. The same interpretive practices that dismiss a Black voice also support framing resistance as a moral failing, while institutional secrecy protects leadership from scrutiny. The result is a combined trauma that affects both individuals and the larger system.

The pattern that emerges from the research and survivors' accounts is clear. Vulnerable and marginalized people are not just more likely to be harmed; they are more likely to experience harm that destroys their sense of self, bodily integrity, and community belonging. They then have to do the difficult work of healing with fewer resources and while facing ongoing suspicion or neglect. Responses that don't understand this layered harm won't effectively help the people who are most affected.

Protecting vulnerability demands intentional reforms that shift responsibility toward care. It requires leaders to embrace ethical obligations that go beyond rhetoric and to establish transparent pathways to validate testimony. It calls on clinicians and community helpers to treat spiritual meaning and racialized experiences as equal domains in recovery. It also involves redistributing interpretive authority so that marginalized individuals do not have to re-earn the right to be believed.

Above all, the survivor viewpoint insists on a moral baseline. Vulnerability should be met with protection, not with predation. The communities that taught people how to trust must be the same ones that stand ready to repair when trust is broken. Until that baseline is restored, vulnerability will remain a doorway through which compound harm is made. Taken together, the quantitative and qualitative evidence support a multilevel model of compound trauma in African American Muslim contexts that emphasizes nested systems and feedback loops. At the macro level, structural racism and Islamophobia create an ambient context of threat and identity vulnerability.

At the middle level, community groups, leadership, and interpretations of beliefs reflect the three pathways described above. At the individual level, members experience a fractured sense of self, physical stress, emotional problems, and withdrawal from others. These individual effects are not just final results; they influence group activities by changing how people take part and share information, and they affect larger community stories over time.

8.2 The Psychological and Emotional Harm

The psychological and emotional damage resulting from the intersection of spiritual abuse and racial trauma is best viewed as a combined wound rather than two separate injuries layered on top of each other. In this integrated perspective, the mechanisms of spiritual coercion and the dynamics of racial oppression reinforce and transform each other, producing a qualitatively different kind of suffering for survivors.

Early frameworks that identified spiritual abuse as an attack on autonomy and spiritual identity are still important, but they may underestimate how racialized power influences what counts as credible testimony, what kinds of shame take hold, and how institutions decide whom to protect. Participants' stories in this study show that these dynamics work together in powerful and varied ways.

One participant described growing up in a congregation where sermons about moral failing were framed in universal language but were applied to her community with a racialized undertone. She said that when she questioned abusive conduct at home or in the mosque, she was told she was being ungrateful and that her complaints would "make the whole community look bad."

The invocation of communal reputation carried both spiritual weight and racial stakes. The message was that raising concerns would not only imperil her spiritual standing but also expose her family to external prejudice. That double bind produced chronic anxiety and a persistent sense of being boxed in. She learned to equate silence with protection for the group and with personal survival. Over time, that adaptation calcified into internalized vigilance that looked like hyperarousal in therapy and excessive self-policing in social settings.

Another participant, a first-generation immigrant, recounted how elders used religious language to explain and downplay racially motivated slights from outside the community. When she tried to describe the emotional toll of both domestic spiritual coercion and public racism, leaders told her she should "offer it up" as a spiritual test. The phrase served as a way to spiritualize marginalization, hiding the underlying structural harm. She said she felt erased and delegitimized. Clinically, she showed symptoms viewed by therapists as depression and somatic pain. However, her way of talking about her suffering was full of metaphors of sin and failing faith. That faith-based language made typical diagnostic categories seem insufficient to fully capture the moral and identity injuries she experienced.

A third participant, a Black woman who had spoken out about relationship abuse in her marriage, described being shamed in ways that linked stereotypes with moral judgments. Gossip and criticism invoked tropes about anger and instability that have long racialized Black women in American life. When those tropes were reinterpreted as spiritual pathology, she faced a double stigma. She explained that members of the elite community viewed her testimony as evidence of spiritual immaturity and as proof of her temperament. The result was social isolation that worsened emotional dysregulation and increased mistrust.

These lived accounts reveal multiple interconnected ways in which spiritual abuse and racial trauma create combined harm. First, credibility issues linked to racialized identities intensify testimonial injustice. Survivors from marginalized racial groups are more likely to be disbelieved or dismissed when they report harm, and when disbelief is expressed with moralistic language, the experience becomes both a moral and epistemic injury. Second, spiritual frameworks that promote forbearance or resilience can serve as racialized coping directives. When leaders encourage patience in the name of faith, they may inadvertently be asking members to endure harms also rooted in structural patriarchal views. This shifts public injustice into a private moral failure, deepening shame. Third, the language survivors use to describe their pain often combines spiritual failings, which hinder clinical understanding and treatment. Symptoms appear as faith-based stories of sin, impurity, or spiritual weakness, while they are also signs of fear, hypervigilance, or complex grief resulting from spiritual harm.

The unique emotional atmosphere created by this combination stands out. Shame in these contexts is not only personal or religious. It also carries the weight of intergenerational stigma and communal vulnerability. Anxiety takes on anticipatory dimensions in which survivors brace for both ecclesial rebuke and social repercussions outside the congregation. Attachment ruptures may reflect not only abusive family dynamics but also a learned wariness toward institutions that have historically protected members of dominant groups at the expense of marginalized persons. These patterns make recovery more complicated because therapeutic care must engage both the spiritual meanings people hold and the racialized structures that shaped those meanings.

Participants who found pathways to partial recovery described healing strategies that addressed both aspects at the same time. One woman mentioned joining a support group where facilitators acknowledged the reality of racialized vulnerability and also helped members reinterpret harmful theological claims. She said that being able to reframe doctrines that had been used to shame her while also recognizing the racial context of her silence restored her sense of moral clarity. Another survivor described therapy that combined pastoral knowledge with culturally informed trauma work. That approach allowed her to separate spiritual language from pathological self-judgment and rebuild trust in her own perceptions.

From both a clinical and community perspective, the implications are obvious. Assessment and intervention need to be integrated instead of separated. Clinicians must have tools to recognize when spiritual language indicates both religious harm and racialized injury. Religious leaders and community organizations must confront how doctrinal rhetoric can uphold racial hierarchies even while claiming moral authority. Without this integrated approach, interventions risk only addressing superficial symptoms while leaving the underlying interconnected harm unaddressed. The stories gathered in this research demonstrate that when spiritual abuse and racial trauma are seen as linked, survivors suffer compounded moral, emotional, and epistemic harm.

Part IV

Mechanisms of Compound Harm

Chapter 10:

Doctrinal Weaponization and Toxic Theology

Doctrinal language and theological frameworks provide communities with moral guidance, identity markers, and shared meaning; they are also social tools that can be repurposed to concentrate power, suppress dissent, and justify harm. This chapter views "toxic theology" not as an abstract moral failing but as the outcome of specific interpretive practices and institutional motivations that turn religious teachings into instruments of control.

Using combined research methods, the analysis follows (1) the ways language and interpretation are used to turn doctrine into a tool for control; (2) the psychological processes, like fear-based beliefs, moral shaming, and taking things personally, that encourage obedience and reduce personal freedom; and (3) common story patterns from survivors that show how harm happens and how doctrine might be fixed. Using theoretical lenses, the injury caused by doctrinal weaponization and toxic theological frameworks collectively shapes both harm and resilience.

10.1 Doctrine as a Tool of Control

Doctrinal control often operates quietly through language and authority rather than through overt force. American community leaders who see themselves as "students of knowledge" claim special rights to read and interpret the Quran and the Sunnah traditions in their original Arabic and within their contexts. As a result, they restrict the space where ordinary American English speakers can question or challenge sacred meanings. The same applies to authoritarian leaders and community Imams in many Islamic communities. When their theological school of fiqh's (madhhab) interpretation is presented as the only correct reading, disagreement is seen as error or deviance, and those who voice concerns lose the credibility to be heard or believed. This concentration of interpretive power makes accountability difficult because challenges to extremism and misconduct are framed as questions of faith rather than issues of harm, and religious defenses can be used under the guise of protecting doctrinal purity (Halonen et al., 2025; Rekis, 2023).

This research's qualitative interviews illustrate these dynamics through everyday interactions that amount to coercion and gaslighting. Participants reported being talked over or having their concerns reframed when they voiced them, indicating that their experiences were not seen as valid grounds for critique. Interpretive authority, usually based on readings of the Arabic texts, becomes a gatekeeping tool—a mechanism that delegitimizes marginalized voices and protects those who benefit from maintaining the status quo. When complaints are labeled as disruptive or unfaithful, members face a double punishment: they endure the original harm and are then accused of attacking the community, introducing new ideas (like innovation or bidah) into the religion, or betraying spiritual norms. This rhetorical pattern reflects classic gaslighting, where the victim's perception is questioned, and the offender's version of reality is enforced.

Doctrinal statements that might offer guidance in other contexts gain profound significance when they are expanded into 'divine' demands. A tentative ethical teaching can be amplified into a claim about salvation, communal belonging, or divine favor, thus portraying noncompliance as haram or a threat to the soul itself. In such a moral economy, silence is redefined as virtue, and disclosure is regarded as sacrilege. Appeals to unity, patience, or forgiveness, therefore, serve as pressure points. They influence how individuals assess their options and make leaving or complaining feel like a spiritual failure.

Instrumental hermeneutics often align with these types of social pressures. Sacred texts are read not to uncover meaning but to support personal or social agendas, such as maintaining a husband's control over his wife or concealing a scandal within the community. Language about forgiveness and reconciliation is used to shut down formal investigations and divert attention from institutional accountability to making private amends. In practice, domestic survivors, usually women, are told to endure, be patient, or preserve the marriage, while efforts that could hold abusers or complicit leaders accountable remain informal, ambiguous, and entirely internal. When power is unequal and safety mechanisms are missing, such appeals protect reputations and reinforce complacency.

Charismatic leadership magnifies these problems because personal authority can be mistaken for spiritual infallibility. When leaders are invested with sacred charisma, their interpretations carry the force of divine mandate for many followers, and congregants may come to equate the leader's directives with God's will. That interpretive chain from text to leader to follower produces relational dependency, and dependency increases the cost of resistance. In the narratives collected, deference to leadership translated into an environment where questioning was discouraged, and where those who questioned were made to feel spiritually defective. The result is not only silence but a culture of compliance that enables further abuses of power.

These processes are intensified by social histories and shared habits of endurance. For African American Muslim communities, teachings on patience and communal unity developed from adaptive strategies of survival and resistance.

These teachings offer meaning and unity, but they can also be misused as commands for absolute submission when institutional oversight fails. Resilience stories thus have a dual nature. They help communities endure hardship, yet they also make it easier for leaders to expect suffering as evidence of faith. In interviews, some participants felt disposable because of how they were treated, a sense that religious knowledge or gender marginality influenced who was seen as deserving protection and who was not.

When doctrinal control, rhetorical gaslighting, instrumental hermeneutics, and charismatic authority intertwine, they produce predictable results for those affected. The mechanisms amplify and deepen harm through several pathways, including the following:

i.   Testimonial silencing that strips survivors of epistemic authority and makes it hard to access help because speaking up is reframed as spiritual failure rather than as a claim about wrongdoing.

ii. Moral confusion and self-doubt that follow from being told that personal advocacy equates to sin, a dynamic that feeds shame and makes disclosure costly

iii. Institutional protection of reputation that directs complaints toward private resolution, thereby limiting options for independent investigation or restorative accountability.

iv. Bodily and psychological effects that arise from stress, somatic symptoms, and identity erosion, because spiritual betrayal worsens other forms of marginalization and leads to a sustained allostatic load (Hürten et al., 2025).

Certain populations bear disproportionate burdens in these environments. Children and elders face demands for trust that are not returned with care, making them especially vulnerable to exploitation and spiritual coercion, even from parents and caregivers. People with disabilities face a higher risk when moral authority is used to override personal agency, leaving them dependent on caregivers who may exploit religious reasoning. For women limited by patriarchal interpretations of scripture, speaking out often comes at a greater cost, and Black women, in particular, navigate an additional layer of racialized disbelief that undermines their credibility and restricts their options for redress (Sharifnia et al., 2023).

On this point, let me add that when doctrine is used as a tool of control and religious patriarchy fosters domestic spiritual abuse, Muslim American children are particularly vulnerable to various developmental and relational harms. They often learn to equate obedience with piety and to suppress doubts or questions about authority, which stifles critical moral reasoning and theological curiosity. Loyalty conflicts arise when children witness a parent being demeaned or silenced, yet are taught to prioritize family unity or religious duty, leading to ongoing cognitive dissonance and emotional stress.

Over time, this pattern can normalize coercion, leading to the internalization of abusive behaviors as acceptable ways to relate. This increases the risk that children will repeat similar dynamics in their own relationships. When caregivers use spiritual language to justify control, attachment processes may be disrupted, leaving children uncertain about whom to trust and impairing their ability to form secure bonds. Academically and socially, children might withdraw, struggle with concentration, experience physical complaints, or face heightened anxiety and shame that hinder learning and peer relationships. The impact is also moral and identity-shaping, as faith can become a source of confusion or trauma instead of comfort, complicating future spiritual engagement and turning recovery into a dual process of psychological healing and theological reeducation.

The psychological toll is intense and specific. Spiritual abuse damages identity, casts doubt on moral worth, and leaves survivors struggling with faith itself. Scholars document strong internal conflicts over trust and self-esteem, feelings often worsened by communal pressure to stay silent. The loss of testimonial authority also forces many survivors into private efforts to reclaim their voice and meaning. That effort can include seeking alternative spiritual communities, pursuing theological education, or finding therapists who understand faith as key to recovery. These paths to healing require resources and social capital that not all survivors have.

Across religious settings, scholars identify similar paradoxes. Patriarchal interpretations of sacred texts can justify domestic violence in some contexts, while faith-based frameworks may also provide empowerment and support in others. Within Muslim communities, ethnographic studies reveal how leaders and institutions can either reinforce coercion or offer refuge, depending on whether authority is exercised with accountability or with domination. Empirical research among American Muslims shows that the rate of domestic violence largely reflects national patterns, but the influence of religious interpretation shapes both the risk and the routes survivors pursue for safety and healing.

Overall, the literature and stories reveal a clear need. Addressing spiritual abuse as a form of control means looking at how doctrine is promoted, how interpretive authority is given, and how institutional incentives favor reputation over individuals. It involves recognizing gaslighting and doctrinal manipulation as harmful, with moral, psychological, and physical impacts. It also means supporting survivors in ways that honor their spiritual importance, restore their voice, and keep them physically safe. Only by facing the interconnected systems of doctrinal control, rhetorical delegitimation, and institutional protection can communities stop sacred language from becoming a tool of oppression rather than a source of comfort and justice.

10.2 Fear-Based Theology

Fear-based theology operates by transforming everyday conflicts and boundary-setting into issues of eternal significance. Survivors in the study described how leaders or family members used scripture, prophetic examples, or tradition to warn that disagreement could lead to divine punishment or social rejection. One participant recalled being told, "You are going to hell if you are not following this way," and he explained that the statement did more than just enforce outward compliance. It fostered a constant inner vigilance where every thought and feeling was judged against an impending spiritual judgment. This anticipatory scrutiny became a lasting form of self-surveillance, influencing decision-making long after the immediate conflict had ended.

Moral shaming worked alongside these theologies to produce social and psychic control. Survivors recounted public rebukes, quiet gossip, and intimate reproaches that together marked dissenters as dangerous or defective. As one participant put it, "They reframed my interventions as evidence of personal instability. They called me 'angry,'" and she traced how that label closed off social support and intensified isolation. Community-level shaming translated into internalized devaluation, eroding the capacity to act and leaving many susceptible to further coercion.

When theological condemnation is woven into self-understanding, the clinical picture becomes intricate and filled with language of faith. Survivors described ongoing self-blame expressed in religious terms, depressive thoughts seen as moral corruption, and physical symptoms that appeared to stem from persistent moral stress. These accounts show how spiritualized shame complicates standard assessment and treatment because spiritual language is intertwined with symptom reports. Therefore, clinicians must address moral epistemic injury and offer interventions that both reduce distress and restore the survivor's sense of being a knowable moral agent.

Fear-based theological framing also spreads through congregations in contagious ways. When disagreement is punished, others learn to keep quiet; institutional silence encourages people to hold back; and shared stories show that resisting has spiritual and social consequences. Studies using numbers in related work connected strict beliefs to less reporting of abuse, and this link was influenced by increased shame. This observed pattern aligns with the interview stories and helps explain how harm continues not only because individual offenders seek to control others, but also because usual practices in worship and community life create situations that prevent people from speaking out.

Participants identified therapeutic and community pathways that helped undo internalized fear and shame, emphasizing that effective healing involves two interconnected tasks. The first task redefines cognitive perceptions of self and spiritual identity so that moral worth is separated from enduring abuse. The second task restores epistemic authority through hermeneutical work, which introduces alternative theological interpretations and diverse readings of scripture. Survivors described narrative therapy, shame-sensitive approaches, and spiritually integrated interventions as helpful because these methods explicitly reframe suffering as a contextually mediated problem rather than evidence of spiritual failure. They also highlighted community-based theological education led or endorsed by survivors and culturally competent scholars as vital for changing congregational norms and creating collective support systems that reduce stigma and encourage help-seeking.

Throughout the interviews, a clear pattern appeared: internal monitoring turns strict religious warnings into constant self-control and reduces personal freedom; being socially excluded because of moral judgment limits access to help and increases loneliness; and using religious language to describe symptoms requires care that respects spiritual beliefs. To address fear-based theology and moral shaming, interventions are needed at the individual, congregational, and institutional levels. These efforts can help restore psychological well-being, reestablish the survivor's authority to interpret moral realities, and transform faith from a tool of control into a source of protection.

10.3 The Role of Spiritual Abuse in Domestic Violence

Domestic violence in faith contexts takes on a distinct and painful form when religion is folded into patterns of control. Perpetrators sometimes draw on sacred texts, theological language, or institutional authority to legitimize coercion in the home and to make abuse feel ordained rather than abusive. Simonič and colleagues documented how religion-related abuse can emerge when spiritual claims are used to justify violence and to silence victims. In such settings, the sacred can be turned into a tool for dominance, and the very language meant to console can become an instrument of coercion (Simonič et al., 2013).

This manipulation can take various familiar forms. A husband may weaponize religious doctrine to demand absolute obedience, portray leaving as sinful, or assert sexual access as a marital right based on scripture. He may use spiritual sanctions to isolate his partner from friends and family, withhold emotional or financial support, or claim that any complaint reflects a failure of faith. Scholars studying Muslim contexts emphasize that patriarchal religious structures can enable this misuse of faith even when core teachings promote dignity and mutual care.

Ethnographic studies reveal that leaders and local institutions sometimes reinforce male dominance, which strengthens a husband's ability to justify control through religious legitimacy.

Religion can also be used in unexpected ways. A spouse might quote religious texts or use social pressure to pressure resources or influence moral judgments against a partner. Such tactics can include threats of public shame in the name of religious standards, claims that a partner is spiritually lacking, or using interpreted traditions to demand material gain. These actions are part of a larger pattern identified by Simonič and others, where theological language is employed for coercive purposes. Both forms of abuse, whether from a husband or a wife, show that sacred authority can be exploited as leverage within intimate relationships.

Empirical studies indicate that domestic violence in American Muslim households occurs at rates similar to national patterns for physical and verbal abuse. Early research found that roughly one in five to one in ten participants reported physical violence, and up to two in five reported verbal abuse, aligning with broader national estimates that one in three women will experience physical violence in their lifetime. Variations across studies reflect differences in sampling and measurement, but the main theme is that household dynamics influenced by religion shape both exposure to harm and how survivors respond.

The presence of religion changes the pathway from harm to help-seeking. Many survivors live in communities where speaking about domestic problems is discouraged or where cultural norms and religious interpretations frame suffering as a private matter or a spiritual trial to be endured. Research by Abu Ras and colleagues highlights how survivors may be pressured to tolerate abuse in the name of preserving marriage or faith, while studies by Chowdhury and colleages and by Istratii and Ali show that communal expectations and religious authority shape survivors' perceptions of their own harm. When leaders and peers frame endurance as piety, disclosure becomes fraught with moral cost, and access to support is limited.

At the same time, faith remains a source of resilience for many survivors. Studies by Istratii and Ali, and by Powell and Pepper, illustrate how spirituality can provide coping resources, meaning-making, and frameworks for endurance and recovery. Some survivors draw on scriptural promises of justice, on prayer to steady their nerves, or on faith communities that offer genuine refuge. The dual role of religion as both a potential source of harm and a resource for healing is a consistent finding across faith traditions and contexts.

This duality presents challenges for Black Muslim women and other marginalized groups whose experiences are shaped by overlapping systems of oppression. Research on the intersections of race, gender, and faith shows that Black Muslim women may face compounded barriers when seeking help and increased vulnerability to spiritual framing of abuse. Younis and others describe how racialization and gendered expectations limit authority and credibility for these women, affecting how their claims are received in family and community settings (Younis, 2009). Qualitative studies with American Muslim women reveal that intersecting identities deepen both the obstacles to disclosure and the complexity of resistance strategies.

The literature also points to particular populations at heightened risk when religion is weaponized. Children and older adults report environments in which trust is demanded but not reciprocated, making them especially vulnerable to manipulation by caregivers or authority figures (Gray et al., 2021). People with disabilities may have their autonomy overridden when religious or moral authority is used to justify control (Sanchini et al., 2022). Platovnjak's framework helps clarify how specific vulnerabilities, such as age, health status, or situational dependence, intersect with anthropological vulnerability, which names our shared human dependence and need for relational meaning (Platovnjak, 2024).

The psychological cost of spiritual abuse within domestic violence is steep. Victims struggle with identity erosion, guilt, shame, and intense internal conflict about faith and self-worth. Captari and colleagues document how these wounds often leave survivors doubting their own moral standing and their ability to seek help without spiritual condemnation (Captari et al., 2024). Hürten and collaborators show that when leaders or institutions exploit trust, processes meant to nurture spiritual growth instead produce control and harm (Hürten et al., 2025).

Taken together, the scholarship and the lived reports reveal a complicated landscape (Ward, 2011). Religion and spirituality can be used to justify and deepen domestic violence. They can also offer pathways to resilience and recovery. Understanding how sacred texts and communal authority are mobilized, whether to oppress or to heal, matters for both research and practice. It calls for interventions that are faith-informed and survivor-centered, recognizing both how doctrine can be misapplied and how spiritual resources can be protective. Addressing spiritual abuse in domestic settings requires attention to the gendered, racialized, and institutional dimensions that shape who is believed, who is protected, and who is left to carry the damage alone.

Chapter 11:

Patriarchy, Gendered Power, and Intimate Harm

Religious patriarchy goes beyond just ideas about gender roles; it is a social system that decides who has power, who works, who is visible, who interprets meaning, and who makes moral choices within faith communities. For African American Muslim women, this system interacts with racial inequalities, histories of gender struggles, and spiritual duties to create unique situations of vulnerability and resistance.

Building on the study's number-based results and detailed personal stories shared earlier, this chapter examines how male-dominated systems in religious groups enable close-up harm, how spiritual abuse manifests in homes and communities, and how the experiences of African American Muslim women reveal both unfair challenges and creative resilience. The analysis uses frameworks of intersectionality, institutional betrayal, and moral-epistemic injury to show how gendered power operates as both a fundamental condition for abuse and a contested space for reform.

11.1 Religious Patriarchy as a Structural Enabler of Abuse

Religious patriarchy in community life often feels less like abstract ideas and more like everyday systems that make male control over interpretation normal. In these settings, the Quran and the sunnah are often understood through male-focused interpretations that strongly support male authority in leading the community and family. When these ways of interpreting become established, they do more than just favor certain voices. They also create standard procedures that deflect complaints, limit accountability, and use official language to justify silence. Researchers have shown how focused gendered power leads to unclear procedures and less questioning. The interviews in this study turn that general idea into real stories of control and betrayal.

One participant described a congregation where the imam and the male board framed all mediation as a question for male Amirs, refusing to involve women in the review process. She said that when she tried to report coercive behavior, she was told the matter would go before a council composed only of men. She described sitting in a room where men had already decided to support the accused and were retelling her story to her. The feeling that no impartial forum existed left her feeling trapped and delegitimized. That account echoes evidence that gendered homogeneity in governance creates both procedural and epistemic barriers to redress (Fricker, 2007).

Doctrinal readings that emphasize male headship and equate female submission with piety provide the moral language that abusers use at home to justify control. One woman explained how her husband quoted passages from the sunnah of Muhammad (pbuh) to demand strict obedience, while pointing to mosque leaders who teach submission as a virtue when she expressed concerns. She mentioned that leaders would advise patience and prayer, framing her calls for safety as threats to marital harmony. The result was that scriptural language was used as a norm to cover behaviors widely recognized in domestic violence studies, such as monitoring, economic restrictions, and social isolation. When sacred texts are read without considering existing power dynamics, they can serve as shields for coercion rather than protections for the vulnerable.

For many women, this patriarchal governance was worsened by racial and transnational factors within leadership. A participant who identified as Black described feeling that her knowledge of scripture was dismissed by elders who were immigrants from other countries. She remembered being told that she did not "understand how to read the religion properly," even as she tried to explain the harm she had experienced. That dismissive attitude carried racial undertones and reinforced credibility gaps that intersectionality scholars have shown to concentrate disadvantages for women of color (Collins, 2000; Crenshaw, 1991). The result was a compounded marginalization that limited avenues for help and increased feelings of isolation.

Institutional responses often compound private trauma. Several participants described leaders who prioritized unity and reconciliation over investigation and protection. In one case, a woman was asked to forgive and reconcile while the husband who harmed her while he continued to attend public events without consequence. She said she felt re-traumatized by the process because the institution had deferred to protecting its image rather than ensuring her safety. That dynamic of institutional betrayal has been linked to worse psychological outcomes and to a loss of trust in communal structures.

Some groups were especially vulnerable within these patriarchal systems. Children, elders, people with disabilities, and women of color faced extra constraints when doctrinal authority was used to override consent or silence dissent (Gray et al., 2021; Sanchini et al., 2022). Despite the heavy influence of religious patriarchy, some survivors discovered forms of theological and community resistance that helped them recover. One participant explained how a women-led study group that taught multiple ways of interpreting the Quran helped members reclaim scriptural sources that upheld dignity and mutual responsibility. She described that work as freeing because it shifted interpretive power away from a small group of men and showed that alternative readings are possible within the tradition. When survivors accessed faith-based therapy or community education approved by culturally competent scholars, they reported greater moral clarity and a renewed ability to seek safety (Captari & Worthington, 2024; Pargament et al., 1998).

The accounts gathered here point to clear structural remedies. Sharing who gets to interpret religious teachings, setting up clear and survivor-focused accountability processes, and building religious understanding that accepts multiple interpretations can reduce how doctrine is used to protect abuse. Without these changes, organizations will keep putting their reputation above survivor safety, and religious language will continue to support control. The evidence and interviews agree on this: religious patriarchy supports abuse, and the resulting trauma affects moral, mental, social, and physical aspects. Addressing those harms requires community institutional reform, theological contestation, and clinical practices that recognize the interlocking nature of doctrinal power and organizational protection (Adams-Clark et al., 2024; Oakley et al., 2018).

11.2 Gendered Experiences Among African American Muslim Women

African American Muslim women's experiences are influenced by mixed cultural and religious traditions and by caregiving and emotional work expectations that are different from those of many other groups. Many participants shared how their journeys to Islam, Black religious traditions, and African American cultural styles shaped how they express their faith and respond to challenges. For some, their background in Black faith traditions provided tools for public criticism and activism; for others, conflicts with international church cultures led to misunderstandings that deepened their exclusion from knowledge and recognition. As one woman put it, "My way of talking about faith came from my Black church experience; when I raised concern, it didn't match the leadership's style, so my voice felt unreadable to them." These hybrid identity negotiations produce both resilience and friction as women contend with multiple interpretive expectations.

Women's disproportionate caregiving responsibilities, organizing events, maintaining social networks, and providing informal pastoral support also increase their exposure to secondary trauma and limit resources for self-care. Several participants noted that because they were regarded as the community's caregivers, their own complaints were often dismissed.

One commented, "I was always the one coordinating meals and taking calls. When I needed help, people assumed I'd manage, so I didn't get the help I needed." These labor expectations cause burnout, limit capacity for recovery, and make women's complaints less visible in congregational life, a pattern consistent with feminist analyses of care work and emotional labor.

Intersectional stigmas further complicate help-seeking. Racial stereotypes about Black women, assumptions of hyper-resilience, invulnerability, or sexualization, interact with religious beliefs that see suffering as a test. Participants also reported experiences of disbelief or being minimized by both secular service providers and religious leaders. One woman recalled being questioned by a counselor who implied she might be "overreacting." Such responses reinforce long-standing patterns where Black women's testimonies are dismissed at the intersection of race and gender, complicating both access to clinical help and faith-based forms of support.

Yet, the narratives also highlight creative ways of agency and community innovation. Participants discussed creating women-led support networks, launching internal accountability initiatives, and rephrasing theological language to emphasize safety and gender equity. One woman who helped start a mosque accountability group shared the slow but real changes that followed: "We started a women's accountability team, wrote safety procedures, and invited scholars to teach feminist readings. Slowly, the mosque began to change how they responded." Such grassroots efforts build on histories of Black women's organizing and faith-based activism, connecting spiritual practice to social justice and institutional change (hooks, 2000; Morris, 2016).

Addressing intimate harm among African American Muslim women requires interventions that are simultaneously clinical, congregational, and structural. Clinically, trauma-informed practices that include narrative repair, shame-sensitive approaches, somatic regulation, and culturally and spiritually attuned theological reframing will better serve survivors' needs than secular models that overlook moral-epistemic injury. Congregationally, diversifying leadership and decision-making, establishing clear, survivor-focused ways to report issues and seek outside reviews, and adding training on trauma and gender fairness to pastor education are important steps toward making places safer. Building community strength by supporting women-led groups, providing legal and financial assistance to community members, and offering public religious education can shift shared attitudes toward responsibility.

Chapter 11.3

Epistemic Injustice and Testimonial Silencing

Epistemic injustice and testimonial silencing are central lenses for understanding how knowledge, credibility, and voice are systematically distorted within religious communities, with especially acute consequences for marginalized members. This chapter explains how testimonial and interpretive injustices operate in congregational settings, documents racialized delegitimization in masjids and community spaces, and traces the cognitive, emotional, and identity-level consequences that follow when members' voices are discounted or erased. Drawing on interviews, field observations, and survey data from the present research study, the analysis foregrounds how race, gender, and religious authority interact to produce epistemic harm and situates those harms within broader sociocultural and institutional dynamics.

11.4 Testimonial and Hermeneutical Injustice

Testimonial and hermeneutical injustice in the masjid context is especially damaging because theological vocabularies and doctrinal traditions often lack the language to describe spiritual coercion or gendered abuse. When communities do not share concepts to identify harm, members find it hard to express their experiences (their testimony) and to get proper responses.

Several women recounted that descriptions of coercive control were reinterpreted by leaders as marital issues or spiritual tests; as one explained, "He'd say 'it's your duty to obey' and when I asked for help, the leaders told me to be patient and focus on my faith, not my rights. The scriptural talk made it feel like I was the problem" (Cana). These interpretive strategies reveal both the limited conceptual resources and resistance to broadening hermeneutical frameworks to include gendered abuse (Pargament & Exline, 2020; Oakley et al., 2018).

Testimonial and hermeneutical injustices reinforce each other. When members' testimonies are not believed, the resulting silencing reduces the creation of shared knowledge about abuse and maintains hermeneutical poverty. Conversely, when interpretive resources are lacking, individuals' accounts are often dismissed as misinterpretation or moral failing, which further deepens testimonial deficiencies. The mixed-methods results from this research support these dynamics. The statistical patterns show that experiences of spiritual harm and race-based stress frequently occur together and are closely linked to distress, conditions that worsen when individuals' testimonies are dismissed (Ramler, 2023).

11.5 Racialized Delegitimization

Racialized delegitimization is a specific type of testimonial injustice where credibility is undermined by negative stereotypes and cultural assumptions related to race, ethnicity, and culture. African American Muslim women in this study often reported that their credibility was damaged by intersecting stereotypes; being portrayed as overly emotional, not religious enough, or, conversely, as unusually resilient in ways that made their suffering less visible.

One participant described the dismissive label she received when she tried to speak: "When I spoke up, they would talk over me or reframe what I said..." (Aneesah). Another participant observed how racial dynamics affected who was believed: "In a mosque where leadership is mostly from another country, I felt my words translated as less valid; it was like they didn't expect people like me to know the religion" (Daliah). These qualitative reports reflect scholarship showing how racialized credibility deficits weaken the acceptance of marginalized testimony in institutional settings (Collins, 2000; Crenshaw, 1991).

Transnational leadership structures can worsen these issues in some congregations. When immigrant leadership teams hold cultural beliefs about gender, hierarchy, and honor that clash with African American congregants' expectations, credibility hierarchies often favor immigrant stories and institutional stability over local voices. Several interviewees described formal judgment processes or reconciliation practices that implicitly prioritized maintaining reputations over survivor well-being; as one participant recounted, "At the meeting the imam kept saying 'forgive and reconcile.' Meanwhile, the man kept showing up at events as if nothing happened. I felt like the system protected him, not me" (Cana). These patterns reflect findings from studies on mosque governance and transnational authority, showing how procedural neutrality can produce uneven and damaging effects (Al'Uqdah et al., 2019; Oakley et al., 2018).

Strategies that enable racialized delegitimization are often subtle and socially reinforced. Calls for unity, forgiveness, or communal duty frequently shift blame onto survivors and protect the institution's reputation, a pattern documented in studies of institutional betrayal and clergy abuse. Research participants reported that such appeals were routinely weaponized to discredit their moral standing and shift the burden of relational repair onto them, thereby causing both testimonial dismissal and material harms, such as denial of access to community supports (McGraw et al., 2019).

Chapter 12:

Institutional Betrayal and Community Dynamics

This chapter explores how organizational structure, governance practices, and daily institutional routines influence whether congregations protect survivors or perpetrators. Building on the earlier presented convergent mixed-methods evidence, psychometric patterns, and interview themes of institutional betrayal, the chapter places individual harms within community dynamics instead of viewing them solely as interpersonal failures.

Its goal is to show how structural features (such as concentrated authority, informal reputational economies, patronage networks, and reliance on volunteers), discursive practices (like doctrinal framing of dissent and unity-as-silence), and gatekeeping processes (including internalized complaint channels and lack of external oversight) create predictable paths to institutional betrayal and, alternatively, what institutional courage looks like in practice.

The chapter unfolds in three interconnected sections. The first examines structural conditions that consistently favor leader preservation and reputational management, showing how these features institutionalize the protection of authority and limit credible complaints. The second concentrates on gatekeeping and complaint processes, including both formal and informal mechanisms through which institutions filter, distort, or silence survivor testimony, and it investigates the psychological and social effects of what participants called the "Holy Hush." The final section presents models and practices of institutional courage identified in the data and current reform literature, emphasizing concrete reforms such as independent review, survivor-centered reporting channels, anti-retaliation protections, and trauma-informed leadership development that break cycles of harm and initiate processes of epistemic and moral repair.

Throughout the chapter, participants' voices are used not just as illustrative detail but as analytical evidence demonstrating how organizational rules and habits are experienced in practice. These lived accounts are integrated with quantitative diagnostics and institutional theory to explain why betrayal happens repeatedly and how lasting organizational change can be achieved. The chapter concludes with practical implications for congregational governance, seminary and leadership development, and policy advocacy, emphasizing that preventing spiritual and racial harm requires institutional design as much as individual efforts.

12.2 Gatekeeping and the "Holy Hush."

Gatekeeping in faith institutions occurs through both formal processes (such as who sits on complaint panels and which thresholds trigger action) and informal practices (such as who is invited to mediate, how accounts are presented, and which interpretive lenses are considered privileged). Research on institutional betrayal and clergy abuse shows how these gatekeeping activities often filter out stories that threaten the institution's stability, effectively protecting leadership and silencing dissent. Survivors experience these processes as layered, culturally influenced barriers that increase the social and emotional costs of disclosure.

Participants described complaint pathways that were intentionally blocked. One participant reported that referral to internal mediators served as a way to deflect and dismiss emotionally: "When I expressed worry to leadership, I was told to be patient and to pray." This routine reframing of grievances as private concerns exemplifies what survivors often call the "holy hush," which acts as an institutional rule that silences critique under the guise of piety and community harmony (Doyle, 2009; Oakley et al., 2018). The "holy hush" operates through various channels: clear warnings to stay silent, social exclusion when complaints are shared, and procedural barriers that make formal reporting difficult or pointless. Quantitative data from the study support these accounts: participants with high scores on SHAS subscales indicating institutional concealment and doctrinal weaponization reported fewer instances of formal reporting to masjid authorities (Koch & Edstrom, 2022). These statistical patterns confirm the qualitative testimony that fear of damaging one's reputation and social retaliation reduces help-seeking. As one participant reflected on the decision to disclose: "I thought about speaking, but I kept hearing 'be patient.'"

Gatekeeping is often justified as protecting community harmony, but its real effects are clear: relying on internal resolution without independent review re-victimizes complainants, extends their suffering, and allows offenders to stay in positions of power (Smith & Freyd, 2014). These outcomes highlight the moral and knowledge-related costs of gatekeeping; institutions that focus more on protecting their reputation than on transparent accountability consistently weaken survivors' ability to be believed and safeguarded.

12.3 Community Accountability and Institutional Reform

Communities can provide comfort and healing, but they can also become sources of harm when gossip, marginalization, and shunning go unchecked. In this study, participants explained how normal social interactions within their community turned neighbors and acquaintances into perpetrators and enablers of spiritual abuse. Stories that initially appeared to be neighborhood talk or well-meaning advice often served as tools of exclusion that increased existing trauma and made accountability nearly impossible. These qualitative accounts align with the concepts of epistemic injustice and institutional betrayal, which describe how testimonial credibility is undermined and how institutions prioritize reputation over people.

One participant described how a rumor spread after he raised concerns about a local leader's coercive behavior. Abdul (these names are pseudonyms used for research privacy) recounted that the rumor initially appeared as a few whispered comments after prayer, then spread to community gatherings and the mosque's group chat. People who had once brought meals to his family began avoiding eye contact and stopped visiting. Abdul explained that the silence felt intentional and suffocating. He described how narratives shifted from questioning the leader to blaming him and his family. The social withdrawal he experienced removed everyday supports that had once helped him cope with stress and made it harder for him to feel a sense of belonging. His story shows how gossip can shift moral attention away from the alleged wrongdoing and onto the person who speaks up, creating a kind of testimonial devaluation that worsens distress (Fricker, 2007).

Aneesah shared a story of everyday exclusion that became a recurring pattern. After she sought help for ongoing coercion, she noticed small but accumulating acts of marginalization: fewer invitations to events, less participation in study groups, and a consistent decline in casual greetings. She described the repeated experience of salaams going unanswered and the feeling that her presence was ignored. Aneesah linked these behaviors to increasing social anxiety and withdrawal. She explained that this marginalization signaled to her that raising concerns could threaten her social standing and relationships. This process of exclusion functioned as a way to enforce conformity and discourage further disclosure. Her experience aligns with research showing that when communities practice epistemic silencing, survivors lose both social capital and opportunities for justice (Oakley et al., 2018; Panchuk, 2024).

Bala recounted a particularly severe form of institutional punishment that followed her refusal to accept an unequal settlement during a private reconciliation meeting. After she declined terms that she judged unfair, she said greeting rituals ceased, and families whispered to their children not to play with hers. Where Bala had hoped for safety, she was instead ostracized.

The community framed her as difficult and uncooperative and, in doing so, turned what might have been a dispute resolution into social exile. Bala linked the sustained isolation to worsening physical and mental health. She reported emergency care for uncontrolled blood pressure and described suicidal ideation at the lowest point of her alienation. Her story exemplifies how shunning operationalizes punishment by removing access to mutual aid networks and emotional support, and how that removal can translate into somatic crisis (Cénat, 2023; Van der Kolk, 2014).

Daliah shared an account that emphasizes institutional justifications for exclusion. After reporting a leader's abusive behavior, she faced a gradual but evident narrowing of her roles and responsibilities. Invitations to join committees ceased, and she was no longer asked to speak at gatherings. Leadership described these changes as efforts to maintain peace and harmony within the community. In reality, these actions signaled that speaking out had social consequences. Over time, Daliah accepted the message that raising concerns could lead to exile and limited access to community resources. Her story highlights how institutional decisions, framed as neutral efforts to uphold unity, can serve as structural penalties that re-traumatize survivors and discourage future disclosures.

Together, these narratives expose three interconnected mechanisms through which communal life facilitated abuse. First, gossip acted as a swift reputation management tool that shifted attention away from alleged perpetrators and cast complainants as the problem. Rumor and casual talk spread quickly from private spaces to public forums, and then into digital circles, where reputations were molded and damage was magnified. Second, marginalization functioned as a normative enforcement mechanism.

By narrowing roles, excluding people from committees, and withholding ordinary social courtesies, communities taught implicit lessons about the costs of dissent. Third shunning served as an institutionalized punishment. Removing mutual aid and social support not only punished the individual but also made survival within that community practically impossible. These mechanisms combined to create structural disincentives for reporting abuse and prioritized protecting the institutional reputation over individual safety. These processes reflect well-established concerns about institutional betrayal and the moral and epistemic injuries that occur when trusted organizations fail to meet basic duties of care.

Survivors in this study highlighted the need for reforms that address both everyday social practices and formal procedures. They emphasized the importance of accessible reporting channels that prioritize survivor safety and confidentiality. They called for training for leaders and active community members in trauma literacy so that casual speech and exclusionary practices could be recognized for the harm they cause.

Survivor participants also called for neutral advocacy roles that operate outside existing power structures and support survivors throughout the process, ensuring procedures are conducted fairly. They suggested transparent communication practices that balance privacy and accountability, allowing communities to see that concerns are addressed seriously without breaching individual confidentiality. These recommendations highlight the dual need for culture change and procedural reform. Trauma-informed leadership training and survivor-centered reporting systems are both essential and mutually supportive.

The importance of creating alternative sources of social support was also a concern for participants in this study, so that survivors do not become immediately vulnerable if their primary congregation withdraws support. Peer networks and mutual aid groups provide practical help and reduce the influence of gossip and social exclusion. Several interviewees described how partnerships between different congregations and external review bodies provided essential independent oversight when intra-congregational processes were affected by conflicts of interest. Restorative approaches were appreciated when they were survivor-led and when involvement was never forced. These practices emphasize survivor consent, prioritize safety over institutional reputation, and align with models that highlight institutional courage and survivor-centered accountability (Adams Clark et al., 2024; Goertzen & Yancey, 2025).

Spiritual abuse survivors urged ongoing theological and ethical reflection within congregations. They asked that sermons and study circles identify how gossip and exclusion function and model alternative moral responses. They emphasized that protecting reputation at the expense of people is not merely a governance failure but a moral lapse that corrodes trust and spiritual meaning. This theological work is necessary to shift communal norms so that people learn to prioritize protection and restoration over silence and reputation management. Such reflection also helps reassert that spiritual authority can be used to safeguard rather than to punish, thereby restoring the reparative possibilities of faith communities.

12.4 Institutional Courage and Restorative Processes

Institutional courage refers to organizational actions that go beyond just following rules and actively work to repair harm, support survivors, and fix systemic issues. Models of institutional courage emphasize quick acknowledgment of harm, transparent investigations, survivor-focused resolutions, and tangible structural changes to prevent future problems (Goertzen & Yancey, 2025). These models view accountability as an ongoing moral duty rather than a one-time public relations effort. Organizations practicing institutional courage accept short-term reputational risks if it means protecting people and rebuilding trust in the long run (Adams Clark et al., 2024).

Restorative processes serve as complementary tools within a framework of institutional courage. They focus on healing and community repair in ways that formal disciplinary actions do not always achieve. These processes emphasize survivor agency and consent. They are facilitated by trained, independent mediators who possess trauma expertise and cultural competence. Common restorative elements include facilitated dialogue that amplifies survivor voices, institutional apologies that acknowledge harm and accountability instead of mere regret, negotiated reparative measures such as policy changes or restitution, and monitoring agreements with specific timelines and measurable outcomes

(Mulvihill et al., 2023; Ortega Williams et al., 2021). Restorative processes are suitable when survivor safety and justice considerations support voluntary participation. They do not replace criminal reporting or protective sanctions when legal action is necessary.

Concrete operational elements strengthen both institutional courage and restorative practice. First, organizations embed safeguarding into governance documents so that protection is not discretionary. Second, they allocate dedicated budget lines for oversight and for survivor supports. Third, they invest in community education about power abuse and racialized harm so that everyday community members learn to recognize and resist behaviors that enable wrongdoing.

Structural reforms support restorative efforts. Reporting channels must be accessible and separate from local leadership to prevent conflicts of interest. External reviews should be committed to in cases of serious allegations (cases involving criminal conduct), making independent assessments routine. Trauma-informed pastoral care and culturally competent mental health referrals are essential supports for survivors during and after processes. Public remedies such as transparent apologies, restitution, and structural reform help repair epistemic and moral injuries by demonstrating that the institution accepts responsibility.

Redistributing decision-making authority is a further mechanism of institutional courage. Sustainable reform often requires the inclusion of survivor and lay representation in governance. Term limits for board members and rotating leadership reduce the concentration of power that can foster gatekeeping. Formal partnerships with advocacy and legal resources create alternative pathways for redress and reduce the pressure on religious institutions to manage complex cases in isolation. These changes reconfigure institutional incentives so accountability does not depend on relationships that can enforce silence.

Symbolic acts are meaningful when they align with substantive change. Public acknowledgment of failure (at the local Masjid level), a sincere apology, and visible restructuring convey moral seriousness. In racially marginalized settings, explicit recognition of racialized harms is essential. Such recognition restores the credibility of voices that were previously discounted and signals corrective commitment to those whose testimony was undermined by prejudice or theological deference (Ramler, 2023).

Institutional courage requires persistent follow-through. Policies must be actively enforced and implementation monitored. Continued resources for survivor support, ongoing trauma literacy training for leaders, and routine evaluation of accountability mechanisms prevent repair from becoming merely performative

(Smidt et al., 2023). When institutions uphold these practices, they foster conditions conducive to recovery and reintegration. Institutional courage redefines organizational responsibility as an ethical framework. This framework prioritizes individual safety, encourages external oversight, and accepts public accountability as a necessary part of moral repair.

Together, institutional courage and restorative processes present a clear model for breaking cycles of harm. Independent review, survivor inclusion, transparent sanctions, trauma-informed care, and long-term public accountability form an integrated strategy. These elements work across governance practices, culture, and theology to transform communities. When applied with consistency, they make institutions safer and more trustworthy. They also connect theological commitments with tangible duties to protect the vulnerable and restore epistemic credibility to those whose testimonies have been marginalized.

12.5 Best Practices for Community Masjids

Community masjids serve both spiritual and social functions. Best practices for these institutions must reflect this dual purpose and address the specific needs of racially minoritized congregants. Safeguarding policies should be developed through collaborative efforts involving masjid leaders, regular congregants, faith-sensitive mental health professionals, and legal advocates. This collaborative approach improves cultural relevance and legal compliance. Policies should clearly define spiritual abuse, sexual misconduct, and racial exclusion. They should also outline procedures for reporting, protect confidentiality, and include anti-retaliation measures so everyone understands what to expect and what protections are available.

Referral ecosystems improve response capacity. Masjids should develop relationships with clinicians who understand faith contexts, survivor-led support groups, and independent external review networks. Formal memoranda of understanding clarify roles and consent procedures. They also set confidentiality boundaries that protect survivors while enabling effective clinical collaboration. Community education efforts should be consistent and diverse. Friday sermons can introduce safeguarding principles. Small group discussions can encourage deeper conversations. Youth programs need to address power dynamics and promote healthy leadership. Educational content should include theological language familiar to the community while also teaching about institutional betrayal and the harms of unchecked authority. This approach reduces defensive resistance and links moral commitments to practical protective actions (Potz, 2019; Walsh, 2020).

Resources determine what a masjid can sustain. Even modest budget lines for safeguarding personnel, training stipends, and survivor supports significantly boost organizational capacity. Funders and umbrella networks can speed up adoption by providing technical assistance, grant programs, and public recognition for congregations that implement strong safeguarding frameworks. Smaller mosques can form consortia to pool resources. Shared training, joint external review bodies, and collective legal consultation help reduce disparities in capacity across congregations (Adams Clark et al., 2024; Perez et al., 2025).

Institutional arrangements require clear structure. Reporting channels should be separate from local leadership to prevent conflicts of interest. External review must be used for serious allegations, making independent assessment standard practice. Procedures for interim safety and criminal reporting should be clearly defined. Trauma-informed pastoral care and culturally competent mental health referrals must be easily accessible. Public remedial actions, such as an accountable apology and specific policy changes, help rebuild trust and address epistemic harms when testimony was previously dismissed.

Evaluation and iterative learning make reforms durable. Simple monitoring metrics are useful and feasible. Examples include rates of reported concerns, time to resolution, survivor satisfaction with processes, and periodic measures of community trust. Short-term longitudinal tracking can reveal trends and identify unintended consequences. Co-producing evaluation frameworks with congregants and survivors repairs epistemic deficits in knowledge production and ensures that reforms answer community priorities (Galatzer Levy et al., 2018; Halonen et al., 2025; Neal Stanley et al., 2024).

Redistributing decision-making authority promotes accountability. Including survivor and lay representation in governing bodies reduces the concentration of power. Symbolic actions matter when they are aligned with real change. Public acknowledgment of institutional failures, a sincere apology with clear remedial steps, and transparent restructuring show moral commitment. In racially marginalized communities, explicit acknowledgment of racial harms is crucial to restore the credibility of voices that were previously ignored. These actions help heal moral and knowledge-based injuries and make it more likely that future disclosures will be received with care.

All of these measures should be rooted in ongoing commitments to trauma literacy, racial justice, and survivor leadership. Implementation will vary and depend on leadership, resources, and interorganizational cooperation. Small, co-produced reforms remain the most promising path to institutional change. They shift organizational norms and governance to prioritize protecting people over reputation. When masjid policies, practices, and culture reflect this priority, survivors access safer support pathways. Communities rebuild trust, and the moral integrity of shared spiritual life is strengthened.

Part V

Healing, Practice,

and Policy

Chapter 13:

Implications

13.1 Clinical Implications

The results of this research highlight that spiritual abuse and racial trauma operate not as parallel, discrete risk factors but as intersecting, institutionally mediated processes that jointly produce profound psychospiritual harm. Quantitative analyses showed large associations between spiritually abusive experiences, race-based stress, and elevated symptoms of depression, anxiety, and moral-epistemic distress, while qualitative narratives elucidated the mechanisms, epistemic exclusion, doctrinal weaponization, and institutional betrayal, through which community practices and leadership authority undermine testimonial credibility, spiritual agency, and communal trust.

Together, these strands redefine clinical work with African American Muslim members (and others at similar intersections) as requiring simultaneous attention to trauma symptoms, moral-epistemic injury, and the organizational contexts that influence disclosure, meaning-making, and access to support. This chapter translates those integrated insights into clinical priorities: thorough, culturally adapted screening for both spiritual abuse and racialized stress; trauma-informed, faith-sensitive therapeutic approaches that explicitly address moral-epistemic injury; strategies to restore spiritual agency and reparative testimonial authority; and practical tools for safety planning, referral, and provider competence. Each section emphasizes the ethical duty to co-create care with community stakeholders, uphold survivor autonomy, and prevent unintentional re-traumatization by pathologizing faith or obscuring the institutional harms involved.

Assessments must go beyond generic trauma checklists to identify forms of harm that are morally and epistemically influenced by religious authority and racialized legitimacy. The strong correlations observed in this study between measures of spiritually abusive experiences and racial trauma, along with qualitative accounts of intra-communal delegitimization, show that failing to screen for both areas will underestimate severity and miss important combined effects. Practically, intake protocols in mental health and pastoral care settings should routinely include brief, validated items that detect doctrinal coercion, spiritual gaslighting, testimonial discounting, and race-related stressors, while distinguishing coercive practices from protective, faith-affirming engagement (Bedi et al., 2025; Walsh, 2020). Since existing instruments (e.g., SHAS, RTS) were not originally designed for African American Muslim contexts, clinicians should, when available, use culturally adapted versions developed through community collaboration and cognitive interviewing, and interpret scores in light of qualitative disclosures about institutional dynamics.

Assessment interviews should be trauma-informed and shame-sensitive, using narrative prompts that invite clients to describe how congregational language, leadership responses, and racialized legitimacy shaped their experience of harm. Such approaches foreground testimonial restoration over fact-finding and reduce risks of re-victimization that occur when survivors are disbelieved or minimized. Clinicians should inquire about consequences that extend beyond symptomatic distress, identity fragmentation, spiritual ambivalence, withdrawal from faith communities, and barriers to disclosure, because these moral-epistemic sequelae are central to recovery and may signal ongoing institutional risk (Pargament & Exline, 2021). Finally, assessment must include safety screens for suicidality and medical crises driven by chronic stress and ensure immediate risk management when needed.

Therapeutic work should combine trauma-focused methods with interventions aimed at repairing epistemic standing and restoring spiritual agency. Standard evidence-based treatments for PTSD and complex trauma (such as trauma-focused CBT, EMDR) are still crucial for managing hyperarousal, intrusive symptoms, and emotional dysregulation; however, qualitative data suggest these approaches need adaptation to address doctrinal weaponization, spiritual self-doubt, and the moral aspects of harm. Therapies that explicitly include narrative repair, validate clients' experiences, reframe internalized spiritual failure as an institutionalized misuse of authority, and rebuild coherent spiritual identity narratives are especially relevant for moral-epistemic injury (Jones et al., 2022; Pargament et al., 2025).

A faith-sensitive therapeutic approach balances respect for clients' religious beliefs with careful awareness of the potentially coercive use of religious language. Clinicians should be open to different treatment methods, seek advice from cultural and religious experts when needed, and avoid treating genuine spiritual beliefs as problems. Treatment methods that acknowledge shame, normalize reactions to betrayal, differentiate personal value from wrongful actions by institutions, and promote self-kindness help reduce feelings of unworthiness and social withdrawal, which increase risk. When appropriate, stepped-care models can start with faith-centered psychoeducation and peer-led support groups and escalate to adapted trauma therapies for severe or ongoing symptoms, thereby integrating community resources while maintaining clinical standards.

Importantly, clinicians should address systemic and collective aspects of harm. Therapists can assist clients in making decisions about participating in congregations, develop advocacy strategies, and, when the client wishes, facilitate survivor-led community dialogues or refer to external review organizations. These strategies recognize that recovery occurs within social and institutional networks and that healing often involves both personal efforts and structural changes.

13. 2 Individual Psychological and Social Implications

This research study documents how spiritual abuse and racial trauma interact to produce profound individual-level psychological and social consequences. At the psychological level, this compound harm often goes beyond a simple sum of symptoms. Survivors describe enduring shifts in self-concept marked by pervasive shame and a sense of internalized unworthiness. These shifts can erode core commitments and beliefs that once anchored identity. The result is identity fragmentation in which religious meaning grows uncertain and prior spiritual certainties become sources of doubt rather than comfort.

Clinically, the study found higher rates of chronic internalizing symptoms among affected participants. Depression and generalized anxiety often persist after the immediate abusive situation ends. Trauma-related hyperarousal and intrusive reexperiencing are common and can continue without proper intervention. These symptom patterns reflect those described in broader research on racial trauma and complex traumatic stress. The study also highlights moral and epistemic distress as key features. Survivors report ongoing harm to their sense of knowledge and moral agency. They describe feeling delegitimized when they try to identify harm. This epistemic injury makes recovery harder by damaging their ability to seek validation and support.

In severe cases, the research identified medical and suicidal crises tied to the cumulative load of spiritual and racial wounding. Chronic stress symptoms such as uncontrolled blood pressure, sleep disturbance, and somatic pain appeared alongside acute suicidal ideation in some accounts. These outcomes reflect the embodied nature of race-based and institutionally mediated trauma and the need for an integrated physical and mental health response.

The social consequences described in the study are equally important. Trust in community and institutional supports declines when places that once offered a sense of belonging become sources of harm or dismissal. Many survivors reported stopping their religious participation as a protective action. However, this withdrawal has its disadvantages. It reduces access to mutual aid networks, spiritual resources, and culturally relevant social supports. Losing these supports results in secondary harms, such as social isolation, decreased social capital, and increased barriers to seeking help.

These subsequent effects heighten mental health risks and complicate recovery. The research also demonstrates how repeated trauma establishes systemic barriers to disclosure and validation. When testimony is met with disbelief or minimization, survivors often conceal their experiences for extended periods. This secrecy increases shame and hinders timely therapeutic or community support. The combination of epistemic discounting and institutional silence can create a cycle where harm intensifies as opportunities for accountability are obstructed.

Additionally, the study highlights the intergenerational and community-wide effects of these harms. Ongoing spiritual and racial wounds alter parenting practices and community involvement patterns. They reshape collective stories about faith, belonging, and safety. Over time, isolated incidents of institutional or interpersonal violations can build into larger patterns of mistrust and disengagement within social networks. This expanding impact emphasizes the need for interventions that address both individual and community levels, focusing on spiritual meaning, racial stress, and institutional betrayal in a coordinated way.

Together, the psychological and social consequences described require more detailed assessment tools, longitudinal studies to monitor chronic issues and recovery, and integrated therapeutic methods. Practitioners and community leaders should pay attention to moral and epistemic injuries as well as traditional trauma symptoms. They should also prepare for the social consequences of disclosure and the practical loss of support many individuals encounter. Only by addressing both the internal wounds and the social disruptions that follow can care fully respond to the full range of harm caused by spiritual abuse and racial trauma.

13.2 Religious Identity

Religious identity is both a private matter of conscience and a public practice shaped by community, history, and power. For survivors of spiritual abuse, reclaiming that identity requires restoration of spiritual agency, defined as the capacity to interpret one's spiritual experiences, to assert those interpretations with confidence, and to rely on one's testimonial credibility within and beyond religious settings.

The qualitative findings from this study emphasize how epistemic exclusion and doctrinal weaponization weaken that capacity, leading to identity fragmentation, shame, and ambivalence about previously held beliefs. Rebuilding a coherent religious identity, therefore, requires interventions that restore testimonial authority, reestablish interpretive access to sacred texts, and revive embodied faith practices that affirm dignity and moral worth instead of instilling fear or guilt.

Clinical practice must start with validating the survivor's account as a moral and epistemic priority because testimonial validation helps address the double injury of interpersonal betrayal and institutional denial described by participants. Validation does more than ease immediate distress; it indicates that the survivor's spiritual perceptions are recognizable and deserving of acknowledgment, a crucial step in rebuilding credibility and trust. Therapist acknowledgment and careful reflective listening create the fundamental conditions for survivors to explore spiritual loss and longing without being labeled as morally or doctrinally flawed.

Another task is to rehearse concrete language and strategies for boundary-setting in faith contexts, as people often report that doctrinal coercion operated through unchallengeable norms of obedience that were rarely open to reinterpretation. Role-play and scripting in therapy equip individuals to state limits, decline invitations that compromise well-being, and communicate needs in ways that reduce the risk of further epistemic discounting (Latif et al., 2024; Plaisime et al., 2023). These practical skills enable survivors to engage deliberately when it is safe and to disengage when institutional dynamics replicate harm.

Reauthoring life stories is crucial for restoring spiritual identity because narrative therapy techniques help people incorporate traumatic events into broader stories of resistance, growth, and moral development. When trauma is reinterpreted as part of a life story rather than the main defining trait of identity, survivors reclaim control over how they view their spiritual biographies and reduce internalized shame. Narrative work often involves clearly identifying moral-epistemic injuries and connecting them to institutional practices instead of personal failure, thus supporting reparative meaning-making.

Rituals and embodied practices can mend ruptures in sacred meaning because survivors' chosen and enacted rituals help rebuild a felt sense of the sacred that isn't solely mediated by abusive authorities. Reclaiming prayer practices, creating reparative rituals to mark losses, or developing new communal rites with trusted peers restores continuity between belief and practice. These actions serve as reparative when performed autonomously and consensually, counteracting the fear-based religiosity that survivors often face. Using alternative scriptural and theological resources is vital to restoring interpretive authority.

Introducing hermeneutical frameworks that emphasize justice, compassion, and human dignity offers survivors sources of meaning that challenge toxic theological interpretations. Clinicians and pastoral allies can connect individuals with scholarly voices and community traditions that showcase African Muslim contributions and interpretive diversity, thereby contesting narratives that undermine Black Muslim theological authority (Abdalla, 2023; Al'Uqdah et al., 2019). Engaging with sources that affirm the longstanding presence and intellectual agency of African Muslims supports historical continuity and helps survivors reclaim a sense of belonging.

Honoring African heritage within Muslim identity offers a specific reparative pathway. Reconnecting to the histories of

African Muslim companions and scholarly traditions affirms collective resilience and challenges the epistemic marginalization that delegitimizes Black Muslim voices. Community based learning, reading circles, and culturally grounded religious education help restore pride and place personal suffering within larger narratives of survival and theological contribution (Neal-Stanley et al., 2024; Nurein & Iqbal, 2021).

When survivors seek communal reconnection, negotiated re-entry is required and must be guided by safety planning. Clinicians should partner with survivors to identify accountable leaders and external supports who have demonstrated institutional courage and a willingness to adopt survivor-centered practices. Collaboration with such leaders is most effective when survivor autonomy, confidentiality, and consent govern the terms of involvement. Where credible reform exists, re-entry may be restorative; where institutions are unlikely to change, therapeutic support should focus on building alternative networks of belonging.

Grief work is also an integral component of restoring spiritual agency because leaving or distancing from an abusive faith community entails tangible losses of relationships, rituals, and social capital. Therapists should explicitly hold and name this grief rather than minimizing it with premature optimism. Attending to mourning enables survivors to honor meaningful attachments while simultaneously constructing new forms of spiritual life.

Recovery from spiritual abuse is both personal and structural. Individual healing gains durability when paired with advocacy for institutional accountability, transparent complaint pathways, and leadership training in trauma literacy. Individuals who engage in community reform initiatives often report restored purpose and enhanced agency, making survivor-led advocacy an important complement to psychotherapeutic work.

In sum, restoring spiritual agency involves validating testimony, building boundary skills, reauthoring life stories, reclaiming ritual practice, introducing alternative hermeneutical resources, honoring African Muslim heritage, planning safe communal engagement, facilitating grief work, and supporting structural reform. These pathways operate together to reconstitute religious identity as a source of meaning and dignity rather than a field of epistemic injury. Clinical and community interventions that center these aims directly address the mechanisms of harm documented in this study and offer concrete routes for survivors to reclaim faith, voice, and belonging.

Chapter 14:

Community-Based Healing

The results of this research also show that spiritual abuse and racial trauma are social injuries that affect different populations and originate from congregational structures, leadership practices, and broader systems of racial legitimacy. Quantitative links between spiritually abusive experiences and race-based stress with psychological distress become clearer when combined with participant narratives that describe epistemic exclusion, doctrinal weaponization, and institutional betrayal as mechanisms that limit disclosure, weaken moral standing, and damage communal trust.

These findings point to a fundamental truth. Clinical interventions and institutional reforms are necessary but not enough. Lasting healing depends on community-centered practices that restore collective testimonial authority, rebuild social capital, and transform the theological and organizational cultures that enabled the harm.

As a result of this research, I have developed what I call the "Prophetic Model of Community Healing," which provides a faith-based framework for guiding community responses. The model draws on Prophet Muhammad's (pbuh) teachings and his lived sunnah of mercy, attentiveness, and protection of the vulnerable, demonstrating people-centered responses that emphasize human dignity and communities' moral responsibility to care for their most marginalized members.

The model is built on three interconnected practices. First is compassion, seen as active mercy and the protection of dignity. Second is attentive listening, viewed as personalized testimony that challenges testimonial discounting. Third is safeguarding the vulnerable through specific protections and institutional bravery. Together, these practices guide community efforts toward both repairing relationships and preventing issues structurally.

Compassion is the ethical soil in which community healing grows. Treating others with mercy and preserving dignity are repeatedly modeled in prophetic teaching and practice, and they are central to spiritual repair. In practical terms, compassion in congregational life must move beyond platitudes and take institutional form. Communities that center compassion create protocols that prioritize survivor safety over reputational preservation, ensure timely investigation of complaints, and allocate resources for culturally appropriate care.

When communities openly practice compassion, they lessen shame and isolation that prolong trauma and help rebuild social networks crucial for recovery. Compassion also involves theological work. Reclaiming interpretive traditions that emphasize justice, mercy, and protecting the vulnerable conflicts with harmful theological views that misuse doctrine to shame or pressure others. This theological reclamation must be collective and educational. It should include mosque classes, sermon series, and study groups that focus on prophetic ethics and the dignity of every individual, especially those who have been hurt by community members.

Attentive listening is the second pillar of my Prophetic Model. Survivors in this study described how testimonial discounting and epistemic exclusion turned private harm into public invisibility. Attentive listening counters these forces by fostering relational conditions where testimony is received with respect and without presumptive reinterpretation. This practice has specific institutional implications.

First, intake procedures and pastoral responses must be designed to handle disclosures confidentially, record accounts accurately, and avoid questions that could retraumatize or judge morally. Second, leaders and lay responders should be trained in shame-sensitive listening and trauma-informed approaches to see survivors' accounts as credible and meaningful while reducing potential harm. Third, listening should be public when it is safe and desired by speakers. Public truth-telling ceremonies and structured community listening sessions, conducted ethically, can create spaces where experiences are validated, silences are broken, and collective memory is built for institutional accountability.

Protection of the vulnerable is the third and stabilizing practice of the Prophetic Model. Prophetic Muhammad's practice affirms the duty of communities to shield the weak and hold powerful actors accountable. Applying this ethic within congregational systems involves establishing clear reporting channels, independent review processes, and anti-retaliation safeguards that are accessible to those with limited social capital or institutional influence.

Protection also involves practical support for people that meets both material and social needs. Past failures to prioritize survivor safety in faith settings often result from institutional incentives that favor cohesion over care. Changing these incentives requires external accountability mechanisms and community-based coalitions that can apply pressure for reform while providing remediation and support for those affected.

Community-based healing also depends on educational and cultural efforts that challenge racial hierarchies within religious spaces. African American Muslim participants in this study described feeling excluded and de-legitimized in local masjids, which worsened their experiences with racial stress and spiritual harm. Therefore, it is crucial that community initiatives focus on anti-racist teaching informed by both Islamic ethics and modern scholarship on racial trauma.

Islamic educational programs that explore the history of African Muslim Sahaba (companions of Prophet Muhammad), highlight Black Muslim scholars, and address intra-faith racism promote interpretive diversity and challenge epistemic marginalization. When educational initiatives are combined with institutional reforms, the result is a theological culture that resists the weaponization of doctrine and supports diverse forms of Muslim knowledge and authority.

Collective resistance is crucial for healing. Community practices that acknowledge harm and pursue redress serve both to repair and to prevent. Public witness rituals, truth-telling forums, and reparative ceremonies make harms visible and validate survivors' claims in ways that private remediation cannot. These practices must be trauma-informed and survivor-focused. They should incorporate restorative elements that highlight accountability, offer apologies when appropriate, and include concrete steps toward restitution and institutional change. When communities engage in reparative pathways, they reduce the social invisibility that enables cycles of abuse to continue.

14.1 Public Education and Advocacy

Community education and coordinated advocacy are crucial tools for transforming congregational cultures from secrecy and reputation management to accountability and collective healing. The mixed methods evidence in this dissertation shows that spiritual abuse and racial trauma persist due to institutional practices and norms that discourage disclosure and prioritize image control. Public education turns empirical knowledge into everyday actions that alter how communities recognize harm, respond to disclosures, and determine which actions are socially accepted.

Educational efforts should therefore be practical, accessible, and culturally grounded. Lay guides describing common indicators of doctrinal coercion and testimonial discounting can help congregants identify problematic dynamics early and seek help before harm escalates. Webinars for leaders and staff that teach survivor-centered intake and confidentiality protocols can reduce secondary injury at the point of disclosure. Toolkits for building independent external review processes and reporting pathways give communities concrete steps to translate ethical commitments into accountable practices.

Public education also helps reduce stigma and prepares communities for change by normalizing conversations about institutional betrayal and racialized legitimacy. When congregations create spaces for informed discussions about institutional failure, the social tendency toward silence begins to change. Accessible materials that clarify the difference between theological disagreement and coercive doctrine help resolve the moral confusion that survivors often face when leaders frame critique as spiritual disloyalty. Educational campaigns can also give bystanders simple, practical responses that protect survivors and preserve evidence, thus breaking patterns that otherwise allow cover-ups and re-traumatization.

Advocacy enhances the impact of education by altering community incentives. Research shows that congregational autonomy can be used to resist oversight and protect reputational interests at the expense of those who are harmed. Building strategic coalitions among faith communities, mental health providers, legal advocates, and funders develops shared capacities that individual congregations rarely have on their own.

These coalitions can pool training resources, run shared external review panels, and coordinate public policy campaigns that tie financial support and accreditation to proven safeguarding practices. Multi-sector partnerships make safeguarding a standard practice rather than a choice and limit any single institution's ability to avoid accountability by citing autonomy or tradition.

Advocacy must explicitly prioritize racial justice because the study's intersectional findings reveal that anti-Blackness and intra-faith delegitimization amplify doctrinal harms. Policy agendas that overlook racialized dynamics risk creating reforms that protect some congregants while leaving others exposed. Effective advocacy, therefore, focuses on measures that diversify leadership, fund culturally specific services, and incorporate anti-racist teachings into religious and leadership training.

Investing in leadership diversification helps alter whose knowledge is valued in theological discussions and complaint resolution. Funding culturally specific services broadens access to trauma-informed care that aligns with individuals' lived experiences and spiritual perspectives. Anti-racist curricular reforms prepare future leaders to identify and address intra-faith exclusion and epistemic marginalization that often silence Black voices.

Education and advocacy are most effective when they are trauma-informed and humility-centered. Interventions that shame communities without offering concrete pathways for change can entrench defensiveness and obstruct collaboration. By contrast, interventions that combine community accountability with technical assistance, training, and resourcing facilitate sustainable institutional transformation. This means pairing public exposure of harmful patterns with offers of support to implement survivor-centered policies, build review infrastructures, and develop culturally competent care networks.

Together, community education and coordinated advocacy create a mutually reinforcing strategy to change the structural and cultural conditions that allow spiritual abuse and racial trauma. Education gives people knowledge and practical tools for recognition and early intervention. Advocacy alters the incentives and accountability structures that guide institutional behavior. When these strategies are combined and centered on racial justice, community-based healing becomes system-facing rather than just person-facing, and institutions are more likely to meet their responsibilities to protect dignity, address harm, and rebuild trust.

14.2 Theological Reclamation

Theological reclamation must distinguish between authoritative tradition and authoritarian misuse, as scholars like Khaled Abou El Fadl have examined. Abou El Fadl points out that Islamic legal and ethical traditions offer a wide range of interpretative options to promote mercy, justice, and moral reasoning. When these resources, particularly the Quran and the Sunnah of the Prophet Muhammad (pbuh), are reduced to authoritarian interpretations, they become tools of control that conceal personal and institutional misconduct under the guise of divine authority. The empirical findings of my dissertation, which document doctrinal weaponization, epistemic exclusion, and institutional betrayal, reflect this concern. Reclaiming theology, therefore, involves restoring the tradition's interpretive diversity and reviving ways of reasoning that focus on human dignity and communal accountability rather than blind obedience (Abou El Fadl, 2001).

A first step in this recovery is to view authority as stewardship rather than domination. Abou El Fadl's work highlights that religious authority in Islam was traditionally seen as a moral trust rooted in ethical deliberation and public welfare. Restorative theology builds on this idea by insisting that leaders exercise interpretive authority with humility, transparency, and accountability. This requires specific institutional reforms. Leadership selection and training should include formal education in ethics, legal hermeneutics, and trauma-informed care to ensure that those who teach and judge are prepared to resist simplistic doctrinal interpretations that silence victims (Potz, 2019; Van Velzen, 2022). When authoritative voices are fostered as deliberative stewards instead of unilateral arbiters, the community is better positioned to hold power accountable and protect those who are vulnerable.

Second, reclaiming theology involves teaching people to recognize multiple interpretations and think critically about religious sources. Abou El Fadl argues that legal texts and classical opinions are products of specific times and places, so understanding their ethics requires focusing on the law's goals, such as justice, mercy, and the prevention of harm. Programs that combine close reading, history, and moral philosophy can demonstrate to people non-authoritarian legal perspectives, as well as feminist and antiracist approaches to interpreting texts.

Study groups, sermon series, and classes that combine expert input with personal stories help communities shift from one-sided teachings to open discussions and shared moral reasoning (Halonen et al., 2025). Similarly, theological reclamation must explicitly address how gendered and racialized exegeses have been used to deny claims to dignity and authority. Works that analyze the relationship between legal authority and gender demonstrate how patriarchal readings can co-opt religious language to subordinate women and legitimize institutional inaction.

Reclaiming, therefore, involves restoring interpretive traditions that historically protected women's rights and emphasized equality before God. This is not about imposing external ideas; it's about returning to traditional principles focused on justice, fairness, and the protection of the vulnerable. Incorporating these ideas into leadership training and community education helps counter strict scriptural claims used to justify silence and control.

Next, reclaiming theology involves changing how institutions interpret religious texts so that the process is open, public, and inclusive of many voices. Once again, Abou El Fadl warns against allowing only a few closed groups to control interpretation because this can protect reputations rather than ensure accountability. Redesigning institutions to distribute interpretive power among committees, community members, and external reviewers helps prevent one-sided readings and provides survivors with formal avenues to be heard.

Including external review and transparent complaint processes supports the moral principles of reclaimed theology. The approach to theological reclamation should promote ritual and liturgical practices that demonstrate protective ethics. Merely recovering texts is not enough if ritual practices continue to normalize behaviors that shame or silence individuals. Reclaimed prayers, rituals, and ceremonies that respect victims' dignity and agency offer healthy alternatives to authoritarian religious practices. These efforts help survivors find spiritual community and show that the community rejects the misuse of religious authority.

Reclamation is inherently linked to accountability and evidence. Moral argumentation must be supported by institutional practices that verify claims and address harms. Community documentation, anonymous records, and collaborative research provide evidence to assess and improve theology. Connecting scholarly discussions about authority with transparent data on how institutions handle abuse allows communities to judge leaders' moral claims based on their actual actions, helping to prevent excuses for abuse.

Reclaiming theology involves centering those who have been historically marginalized in interpretive processes. Abou El Fadl's emphasis on moral imagination encourages practices that amplify the voices of women, racialized Muslims, and other marginalized groups as legitimate co-interpreters. Developing curricula collaboratively and including survivors in creating teaching materials help fill knowledge gaps and produce theological resources that acknowledge both the harmful and healing potentials of doctrine.

Finally, theological reclamation is a long-term, transformative effort that combines scholarship, pastoral practice, and community governance. It uses the tradition's ethical scope to shift authority toward the Prophetic model of community healing, emphasizing compassion, justice, and protection rather than maintaining institutional power. By drawing on critical insights from analyses of authoritative and authoritarian discourses, scholars and practitioners can design reforms that remain true to Islamic ethics while firmly opposing the misuse of scripture for control. When properly institutionalized and rooted in community co-production, these reforms can rebuild trust, heal moral injuries, and restore religious communities as genuine places of spiritual belonging and collective responsibility.

Chapter 15:

Policy Recommendations

The combined results of this research show the need for policy changes and broad system improvements to address spiritual abuse in racially marginalized faith communities as a public health issue involving multiple factors. Quantitative links between spiritually abusive experiences and racialized stress associated with increased psychological distress are deepened by qualitative themes such as epistemic exclusion, doctrinal weaponization, and institutional betrayal. Together, these lines of evidence show that individual clinical responses and isolated congregational reforms are insufficient unless they are supported by public policy, funding priorities, and regulatory frameworks that realign organizational incentives and the distribution of resources.

This chapter outlines policy directions focused on (a) reframing spiritual abuse and racial trauma as interconnected social factors that influence health; (b) building sustainable faith–health partnerships and reallocation of funds toward culturally relevant services; (c) establishing safeguarding standards tailored to the specific roles of mosques and community groups; and (d) clarifying legal and regulatory pathways that protect survivors while respecting the legitimate claims of congregational autonomy. Throughout these areas, the chapter emphasizes intersectionality, community co-production, and initiatives prioritizing survivor voices and safety over merely maintaining institutional reputation.

15.1 Intersectional Public-Health Concern

Framing spiritual abuse as an intersectional public health issue shifts its category from a private or solely theological problem to a societal condition that causes measurable harm across populations. The study's consistent results show that spiritual abuse and racial trauma do not operate separately. Instead, they intersect to increase psychological distress, reduce access to culturally appropriate supports, and weaken community resilience.

Viewed this way, moral epistemic injury and institutional betrayal act as social determinants of mental health, influencing both exposure to harm and recovery paths. An intersectional public health approach emphasizes how race, gender, and religious identity together create vulnerability and guide policy and practice toward groups whose testimonial authority and social buffers are consistently limited, such as African American Muslims.

Conceptually linking spiritual abuse to public health reveals several important implications. First, it highlights the need for measurement. Population health tools and community assessments must include indicators of moral harm, institutional betrayal, and forced religious beliefs, so that estimates truly reflect the experiences described in the dissertation. Second, it calls for detailed health research that does not treat faith communities as a monolith. Long-term, combined research methods that examine experiences across race, gender, and religious background are essential for generating evidence to fairly distribute resources and develop culturally appropriate interventions. Third, it requires that monitoring and outreach efforts be developed in partnership with the communities involved to avoid repeating the knowledge gaps that cause undercounting and mistrust.

Working with communities on data increases involvement and ensures that statistics and needs assessments align with community priorities rather than outside ideas. Putting this approach into policy and programs means including spiritual abuse in trauma-aware public mental health plans and in the main parts of public health work. Public health agencies can encourage cooperation among medical, religious, and community groups by funding programs that both ease symptoms and support institutional change.

This book stresses that individual clinical care alone is not enough, as community structures and leadership practices greatly impact individual outcomes. Policies that combine therapy access with congregational safeguarding supports and community education provide synergistic benefits for population wellbeing. Operational policy tools include implementing culturally specific outreach strategies and ensuring that data collection processes are developed with community partners. These practices respect confidentiality preferences and generate practical data for resource allocation. Funding priorities should focus on health research that disaggregates harms by race, religion, and gender.

System change also involves reshaping organizational incentives so that safeguarding becomes standard practice rather than an optional program. Regulatory frameworks can link funding, accreditation, or public recognition with transparent reporting systems, independent review processes, and protections against retaliation. Legal and policy reforms that protect complainants and require institutions to demonstrate survivor-centered accountability challenge the structural conditions that the dissertation highlights as key drivers of harm.

At the same time, public health partnerships with faith-based organizations can offer technical assistance, combining compliance efforts with capacity building rather than just punishment. Embedding racial justice within this public health approach is crucial. Intersectional analysis shows that anti-Blackness, intra-faith delegitimization, and gendered marginalization influence both exposure to spiritual abuse and the chances of receiving proper care.

Policy responses that ignore racialized dynamics risk producing reforms that protect some congregants while leaving others vulnerable. Targeted funding for culturally specific survivor services, leadership diversification initiatives, and antiracist curricula in leadership formation address the structural roots that render particular groups more susceptible to doctrinal weaponization and testimonial discounting.

Framing spiritual abuse as a public health issue also changes the language of advocacy. It enables appeals to population wellbeing and to the prevention of downstream costs in mental health care, social services, and civic participation. Public health metrics make it possible to show how institutional betrayal undermines trust and reduces social capital, with implications for community cohesion and for utilization of preventive services.

These metrics can be powerful tools for persuading policymakers, funders, and health systems to adopt prevention-focused approaches that emphasize dignity and accountability alongside clinical care. Ethical implementation of this framework requires humility and partnership. Data collection and surveillance should be designed to protect confidentiality and prevent re-traumatization. Interventions must be trauma-informed and culturally responsive, developed collaboratively with survivors and community leaders to reflect lived priorities. Evaluation should be iterative and transparent, allowing reforms to be refined based on community feedback and evidence of effectiveness rather than top-down assumptions (Galatzer Levy et al., 2018; Neal Stanley et al., 2024).

An intersectional public health framing situates spiritual abuse within the broader architecture of social determinants of health. It makes visible the ways in which moral epistemic injury and institutional betrayal operate at scale, and it provides a pragmatic pathway for policy action. By combining improved measurement, community co-produced research, targeted funding, multilevel interventions, and accountability-oriented regulatory levers, public health approaches can reduce harms, enhance access to culturally congruent support, and strengthen communities' collective capacity to prevent and respond to spiritual abuse. This approach preserves respect for religious freedom while insisting that the safety, dignity, and epistemic standing of congregants be fundamental public health priorities (Adams Clark et al., 2024; Halonen et al., 2025; Neal Stanley et al., 2024).

Part VI

Future Directions

Comparative Studies Across Faith Traditions

Comparative research across faith traditions and marginalized communities reveals a striking gap in scholarship, especially regarding African American Muslims and Black and other marginalized people more broadly. Spiritual abuse and racial trauma are increasingly recognized as serious harms, yet studies that examine their combined impact remain rare. Much of the existing literature concentrates on spiritual abuse in predominantly White Christian settings, which has generated valuable insights but also left methodological and representational blind spots that limit culturally responsive care (Fernández, 2022).

In contrast, the experiences of African American Muslims facing combined spiritual and racial harm are not well documented in academic research or healthcare, leaving professionals and communities without specific ways to understand and address these overlapping issues. Studies that focus on combined and culturally based approaches show how spiritual abuse and racial trauma can strengthen each other in situations where racial bias affects who is trusted and supported.

Studies by Ahmad et al. (2024) and Al'Uqdah et al. (2019) describe authoritarian leadership, fixed gender roles, and racial exclusion in some Muslim communities that are seen as religious purity. Quantitative survey work by Mogahed and Ikramullah (2020) comparing Black and White Muslims shows that African

American Muslims experience more religious exclusion and spiritual rejection than other minority groups. These findings suggest that race and religion often combine to increase distress in ways that looking at only one factor will miss. Comparative studies, therefore, help both to test if ideas developed in main contexts apply more widely and to uncover specific causes of harm and strength.

Fair and balanced scholarly comparative inquiry is important because unfair comparisons that miss essential cultural differences in how harm is experienced are clinically detrimental to diverse populations. Comparing different religious groups also helps us understand better. Institutional features such as leadership levels and theological doctrines that focus on sin and forgiveness can affect how moral harm occurs in Black churches, African American Islamic mosques, Hispanic Catholic parishes, and evangelical megachurches (Oakley et al., 2018; Pargament & Exline, 2020).

Finding ways for communities to reduce harm helps develop effective best practices and guide policy recommendations that benefit every tradition. For example, leadership shared among many people and racially diverse leadership groups may lessen the link between strict rules and mental stress, while leadership controlled by a few people could make it easier for people to be ignored or doubted when they speak up.

The comparative perspective has clear practical implications for clinicians, faith leaders, and community advocates. Mental health professionals can utilize evidence from various settings to develop trauma-informed, culturally responsive care that addresses both spiritual and racial contexts. Religious communities can apply comparative findings to enhance safeguarding, transparency, and survivor-centered accountability practices. Funders and policymakers can prioritize investing in culturally specific survivor services and partnerships that integrate faith and health sectors, thereby expanding access to support systems that mirror the lived realities of marginalized congregants.

Comparative research also carries an ethical obligation. Centering marginalized voices corrects past omissions and produces knowledge that is both scientifically strong and justice-focused. When studies intentionally include and highlight the perspectives of African American Muslims and other underrepresented groups, they not only enhance the validity of concepts like epistemic exclusion and doctrinal weaponization but also build a foundation for interventions that restore voice, dignity, and trust. In this way, comparative work pushes trauma discourse beyond isolated variables and toward frameworks that address the interconnected social and psychological aspects of harm.

Conclusion

Reclaiming Faith and Resisting Harm

A circle formed in the community center after the study results were shared. Around the table sat survivors, an Imam who had begun questioning his own training, a clinical psychologist who had worked with racialized clients for decades, a youth organizer, and a scholar who had focused on religious authority. Their conversation unfolded like a slow unpeeling of what had been learned over the past week and throughout the research. Each voice braided personal experience with collective strategy and theological reflection so that the conversation moved from testimony to concrete plans for reclaiming faith while everyone agreed with one voice to resist spiritual abuse and intra-racial harm.

A survivor began by describing how the first step toward reclaiming faith was naming what happened. She said that when her pain was labeled as spiritual failure, she internalized blame and withdrew from community life. When someone helped her reframe the harm as institutional betrayal, she felt relief and clarity. The psychologist responded that clinical work must honor that shift. Therapy cannot only reduce symptoms; it must also restore testimonial authority and support survivors in reclaiming spiritual agency. Clinical practices that combine trauma awareness with faith sensitivity enable survivors to hold on to spiritual meanings that sustain them while disentangling those meanings from coercive leadership practices.

The Imam spoke next, expressing a mix of humility and determination. He explained that his own training had focused on obedience and doctrinal authority and that he had not been taught to see how legalistic rhetoric could be weaponized. He had started to turn to interpretive resources within the tradition that highlight mercy, justice, and the well-being of the vulnerable. He argued that reclaiming faith requires leaders to show interpretive humility and to invite scrutiny rather than assume institutional infallibility. The scholar at the table added that Islamic tradition contains multiple interpretive streams and that recovering those streams is a theological task as well as an institutional one. He urged that seminaries and leadership programs include courses on moral hermeneutics, gender justice, pastoral care, and the ethics of authority so future leaders are prepared to exercise stewardship rather than domination.

The youth organizer raised a practical concern about access and inclusion. Young people and marginalized congregants often feel epistemically discounted and are thus less likely to report harms. She described plans for peer-led support spaces and for survivor-facilitated study groups where lived testimony would be central rather than peripheral. These spaces could teach communities how to read sacred texts in ways that foreground compassion and accountability and could create alternatives for those who did not feel safe returning to previous institutions.

The clinician and the survivor together sketched how therapeutic and communal repair could be braided. They imagined reparative rituals that offer public witness and communal grieving while protecting survivors from further exposure if they prefer privacy. They emphasized that ritual and liturgy could be redesigned to affirm agency and dignity so that worship itself becomes a corrective to practices that had previously shamed or silenced people. The Imam offered to pilot a sermon series that would pair scriptural exegesis with survivor stories and with concrete explanations of safeguarding policies. He saw this as a step toward aligning theology with ethics in ways that were visible and accountable.

The discussion then moved to institutional mechanisms. The scholar argued that restoring faith required reallocating interpretive authority through accountable organizations and transparent processes. He suggested establishing external review panels that include survivors and community members, along with multi-channel reporting systems so disclosures are not handled solely by a single leader. The youth organizer and the survivor stressed the importance of co-creation. They insisted that any reform, educational program, or research project be designed with those most affected in mind, rather than being imposed on them. Co-produced curricula, survivor advisory boards, and community-guided data practices were recommended as ways to avoid repeating patterns of epistemic exclusion.

A public health perspective naturally entered the conversation when the psychologist reminded everyone that spiritual abuse and racial trauma are not just personal wounds. They influence population health and social factors that affect mental well-being. She suggested incorporating measures of moral epistemic injury into community health assessments and called for funding long-term studies that observe how institutional practices impact recovery over time. The Imam and the youth organizer welcomed this approach because it translated community needs into language that could motivate local health departments and foundations to support multi-level interventions combining clinical care, congregational reform, and public education.

When the topic of intra-racial harm and anti-Blackness came up, the atmosphere at the table became serious and honest. Survivors described how delegitimization often appeared in racialized ways and how gendered power dynamics increased vulnerability. The scholar and the clinician agreed that anti-racism must be at the heart of all reform efforts. They proposed leadership diversification initiatives, funding for culturally specific services, and anti-racist education in leadership development. The imam acknowledged the discomfort of confronting group biases and committed to supporting listening sessions and facilitated dialogues focused on accountability instead of shame. These discussions would be organized to amplify Black voices and explore historical and current power dynamics that had often gone unaddressed.

Practical considerations arose as the group discussed the tension between protecting religious freedom and ensuring safety. The youth organizer observed that reforms are more sustainable when paired with resources and technical support. The scholar suggested using incentives instead of relying solely on sanctions. For example, grant-making organizations and denominational networks could link public benefits to demonstrated safeguarding practices and transparent reporting. The psychologist warned that incentives should be designed to prevent token compliance and encourage real institutional change. Evaluation metrics and community feedback loops were proposed as ways to ensure accountability stays meaningful.

The survivor voices emphasized that repair must include material support. Long-term well-being relies on economic stability and peer networks as much as on psychological care. They described mutual aid collectives, mental health counseling services, and community funds that offer practical assistance during and after disclosure. The imam suggested using the masjid as a potential location for hosting such resources, provided that governance structures were adjusted to ensure individual safety and confidentiality. He agreed that institutions should not only apologize when harms are exposed but also demonstrate repair through tangible supports and clear changes to governance and educational practices.

As the discussion shifted to action steps, the group expressed a shared ethic guiding each proposal. They confirmed their commitment to the spiritual values that draw people to community life. They also committed to moral accountability as a theological obligation. Restoring trust involves both protecting dignity and creating systems that prevent power from being used as a shield. The psychologist summarized by saying that reclaiming faith and preventing harm are mutually reinforcing goals. When communities establish transparent institutions, when leaders are trained in humility and trauma awareness, and when survivors are prioritized in education and governance, spiritual life can flourish without recreating coercive authority.

The meeting concluded with plans rather than clear answers. They agreed to test a community-led curriculum that combined theological reflection with trauma literacy and power analysis. They planned a public education campaign to turn research into accessible guides and workshops. They committed to creating an external review body accountable to survivors and seeking funding for long-term research to monitor outcomes. Every participant recognized that the work ahead required humility, endurance, and ongoing partnership with those most affected.

It hasn't been too long since this meeting, and I look forward to the weeks that follow to begin the pilot initiatives that will bear early fruit. I look forward to witnessing how study groups open new avenues for interpretation and help some congregants re-engage with worship and other acts of ibadah on their own terms. I look forward to the cohort of leaders completing training in trauma-informed pastoral care and reporting changes in how they handle disclosures. I look forward to seeing community-led support networks provide immediate practical assistance to people leaving harmful settings. None of these changes were panaceas. The group acknowledged that deeply rooted patterns of authority and marginalized exclusion take time to shift. They also celebrated that the interaction between theological reclamation and institutional reform created pathways for healing that honored both spiritual meaning and moral accountability.

This collective effort demonstrated a key lesson of the research. Reclaiming faith and resisting harm are not mutually exclusive goals. They require collaborative work among survivors, leaders, clinicians, scholars, and organizers. Each role offers essential expertise and moral witness. When this work is based on co-production and a clear commitment to anti-abuse and accountability, communities can protect spiritual values while dismantling the structures that enabled spiritual abuse. The process is iterative and relational, demanding long-term commitment. Yet, the discussion at that table made clear that when people come together with honesty and care, faith can be reclaimed as a source of refuge and resilience rather than a tool for control and silence.

Final Reflections:

These reflections emerge from a place shaped by two vocations and countless encounters. I once stood as a Christian minister, and now I stand as a devout Muslim and a scholar who has spent years listening to survivors, sitting with their tears, and tracing the patterns that link spiritual abuse with racialized harm. This research has been rigorous and at times gut-wrenching. It has shown how toxic theology, patriarchal authority, and institutional protectionism can wound souls and erode trust. Yet alongside the testimony of harm, I have borne witness to persistent and luminous resilience. That resilience is not merely human grit. It is rooted in trust in Allah and in the Names by which He comforts, opens, forgives, and heals.

Loving Islam in this context is not just sentimental admiration for doctrine disconnected from real life. For me, the love of Islam is renewed every day through engaging with the tradition as a way of healing. When people describe their pain as moral and epistemic injury, I think of Allah Al Fatah, the One who opens. The Opener. That Name reminds me that openings happen even in the tightest constraints. An opening could be an imam who chooses humility over reputation. It could be a survivor-led support group that refuses to stay silent. It might be a policy change that calls for transparency and external review. To love Islam is to trust that the tradition offers pathways to justice and healing, and to work to uncover those paths where they have been hidden.

Loving Islam and the Muslims involves recognizing Allah as Ar-Rahman. When Allah's mercy guides our responses, it is not a soft alternative to accountability but a force that affirms human dignity and fosters healing. In clinical practice, mercy means offering compassionate care that respects spiritual significance while addressing harm. In community life, mercy involves establishing procedures that encourage disclosure and protect the vulnerable. In scholarship, mercy entails rejecting narratives that reduce people to objects of study and instead amplifying their voices in ways that restore their agency. Loving Islam means practicing mercy so that theological speech becomes a form of care rather than a means of control.

When I think of Al Ghafoor (The Most Forgiving Lord, who loves to forgive), it evokes the possibility of my forgiving other community members when it is freely given and properly reestablished. Forgiveness in the face of personal or institutional betrayal is complex; let's be honest. It is not a demand that eliminates accountability. It can be a personal act that goes hand in hand with ongoing efforts for institutional repair. To love Muslims is to acknowledge the challenges of forgiveness when harms remain unresolved and to support others in choosing their own paths. It also means encouraging communities and leaders to pursue genuine reform that makes forgiveness possible in the future. The presence of Al Ghafoor in our stories of repair reminds us that forgiveness and accountability can coexist when community institutions accept responsibility and take concrete steps to change.

I cannot reflect on healing from abuse without considering how Ash-Shafi addresses the inner work of healing and curing. Many people I interviewed described wounds to the heart and spirit that traditional clinical categories find difficult to fully capture. Some literature calls it 'Soul Murder' (McPhillips, 2018; Shengold, 1989). The idea of moral epistemic injury helps identify those wounds, but simply naming them is not enough. Healing requires approaches that address the soul as well as symptoms. Faith-based therapy, ritual practices that enable communal grieving, and reparative liturgies can all help restore emotional balance. To love Islam is to trust that the tradition contains resources for holistic healing, and to love Muslims is to support practices that foster that healing.

These theological anchors shape how I see ethical responses. My research shows that spiritual abuse rarely occurs alone. It is connected to racialized delegitimization and larger social structures that determine who is believed and protected. Therefore, committing to loving Muslims means taking a strong stance against marginalization. It involves listening more attentively to African American Muslims and other marginalized voices. It also requires providing resources for culturally specific services and holding leaders accountable for patterns of testimonial discounting. Our love cannot be purely spiritual while ignoring the material and discursive conditions that cause harm.

As a practical matter, this love manifests in specific actions that are both humble and courageous. It appears in leaders who invite outside scrutiny and model interpretive humility. It appears in clinicians who combine trauma-informed care with faith sensitivity. It involves individuals reclaiming control over how their stories are used in research and reform. It shows communities pooling resources to support those leaving abusive environments. None of these acts are easy. They require sacrifice, patience, and ongoing learning. They are, however, expressions of a love that takes suffering seriously and refuses to accept it as normal.

My research shows that faith remains strong when connected to justice. Loving Islam does not mean avoiding critique. It represents a commitment to the core ethical principles of the tradition. Loving Muslims involves embracing both compassion and accountability. It means refusing to choose between spiritual values and moral progress. It means holding onto hope in Allah even while working tirelessly to reform human institutions that have let down some of His followers.

Every time a survivor shared with me the moment they were believed, I felt that opening. Every time a community implemented a new safeguarding measure, I heard the echo of mercy. Every time a leader took responsibility and started to change, I saw the possibility of forgiveness reemerge. These moments are small but meaningful. They testify to the enduring qualities of Allah. My love for Islam is therefore an active love. It is a love that studies, listens, confronts injustice, and seeks repair. My love for Muslims is rooted in companionship with those who have been wounded and those who work for transformation. In this work, I am humbled by the trust placed in me by participants and buoyed by a deep hope in Allah. That hope sustains the belief that when mercy meets accountability, communities can reclaim spiritual treasures, restore dignity, and allow faith to flourish as a refuge and a source of justice.

References

Abdalla, M. I. (2023). "My Islam be Black": Resisting erasure, silence, and marginality at the intersection of race and religion. Communication, Culture & Critique, 16(1), 9–16.

Abou El Fadl, K. M. (2001). *And God knows the soldiers: The authoritative and authoritarian in Islamic discourses.* Bloomsbury Publishing PLC.

Ahmad, S. S., Hammad, I., Rbeiz, K., Ebrahimi, C. T., Alshabani, N., McLaughlin, M. M., Kia-Keating, M., & Weisman de Mamani, A. (2024). Exploring cumulative identity-based discrimination, distress, and traumatic exposure among Muslims living in the United States. Psychological Trauma: Theory, Research, Practice, and Policy. Advance online publication.

Ahmad, S. S., McLaughlin, M. M., & Weisman de Mamani, A. (2022). Spiritual bypass as a moderator of the relationships between religious coping and psychological distress in Muslims living in the United States. *Psychology of Religion and Spirituality.* Advance online publication.

Alcalá, H. E., & Sharif, M. Z. (2018). Islamophobia, health, and public health: A systematic literature review. *American Journal of Public Health, 1*08(6), e1–e9.

Alessi, E. J., & Kahn, S. (2022). Toward a trauma-informed qualitative research approach: Guidelines for ensuring the safety and promoting the resilience of research participants. *Qualitative Research in Psychology, 20*(1), 121–154.

Al'Uqdah, S. N., Hamit, S., & Scott, S. (2019). African American Muslims: Intersectionality and cultural competence. *Counseling and Values, 64*(2), 130–147.

Alvidrez, J., & Tabor, D. C. (2021). Now is the time to incorporate the construct of structural racism and discrimination into health research. *Ethnicity & Disease, 31*(Suppl 1), 283.

Andresen, F. J., Monteith, L. L., Kugler, J., Cruz, R. A., & Blais, R. K. (2019). Institutional betrayal following military sexual trauma is associated with more severe depression and specific posttraumatic stress disorder symptom clusters. *Journal of Clinical Psychology, 75*(7), 1305–1319.

Awaad, R., & Riaz, T. (2020). Insights into the psychological sequelae of spiritual abuse. In the Hurma Project Research Conference, Chicago, IL.

Aziz, S. F. (2012). From the oppressed to the terrorist: Muslim-American women in the crosshairs of intersectionality. *Hastings Race & Poverty Law Journal, 9*, 191.

Aziz, S. F. (2022). The racial Muslim: When racism quashes religious freedom. University of California Press.

Bassioni, R., & Langrehr, K. (2021). Effects of religious discrimination and fear for safety on life satisfaction for Muslim Americans. *Journal of Muslim Mental Health, 15*(1).

Bauer, G. R., Churchill, S. M., Mahendran, M., Walwyn, C., Lizotte, D., & Villa-Rueda, A. A. (2021). Intersectionality in quantitative research: A systematic review of its emergence and applications of theory and methods. SSM — *Population Health, 14*, 100798.

Bedi, R. P., Douce, T. B., Dreier, V. R., & Cardona, B. (2025). Integrating clients' religion/spirituality into practice: A comparison between psychologists, counselors, marriage and family therapists, and clinical social workers in Colorado. *Journal of Clinical Psychology, 81*(10), 964–972.

Bonelli, R. M., & Koenig, H. G. (2013). Mental disorders, religion and spirituality 1990 to 2010: A systematic evidence-based review. *Journal of Religion and Health, 52*(2), 657–673.

Captari, L. E., Choe, E. J. Y., Stein, L. B., & Sandage, S. J. (2024). Trauma survivors' spiritual struggles and the anger of hope: A practice-based clinical study examining links with mental health symptoms and well-being. *Spirituality in Clinical Practice, 11*(3), 235–249.

Captari, L. E., & Worthington, E. L., Jr. (2024). Assessing and treating trauma impacts in religious and spiritual populations: Introduction to the special issue. *Spirituality in Clinical Practice, 11*(3), 195–202.

Cashwell, C. S., & Swindle, P. J. (2020). When religion hurts: Supervising cases of religious abuse. In Trauma-Informed Supervision (pp. 180–203). Routledge.

Cénat, J. M. (2023). Complex racial trauma: Evidence, theory, assessment, and treatment. *Perspectives on Psychological Science, 18*(3), 675–687.

Chen, T. H., Sun, Y. L., Tsai, D. C. W., Huang, Y. M., & Zhang, S. (2024). Diagnosing and mitigating multicollinearity in moderated multiple regression. *YMC Management Review, 17*(1), 9–22.

Chowdhury, R., Winder, B., Blagden, N., & Mulla, F. (2022). "I thought in order to get to God I had to win their approval": A qualitative analysis of the experiences of Muslim victims abused by religious authority figures. *Journal of Sexual Aggression, 28*(2), 196–217.

Çınaroğlu, M. (2024). Islamic coping, post-traumatic stress disorder (PTSD), and Islam-oriented trauma-focused cognitive behavioral therapy (IO-TF-CBT) in the post-Kahramanmaraş earthquake period. *Eskiyeni, (52)*, 351–376.

Cole, M. (2023). Psychological effects of Christian teachings about sin and hell. Mental Health, *Religion & Culture, 26*(8), 736–754.

Crenshaw, K. (1989). Demarginalizing the intersection of race and sex: A Black feminist critique of antidiscrimination doctrine, feminist theory, and antiracist politics. University of Chicago Legal Forum, 1989(1), Article 8.

Crenshaw, K. (1991). Mapping the margins: Intersectionality, identity politics, and violence against women of color. Stanford Law Review, 43.

Creswell, J. W., & Plano Clark, V. L. (2017). Designing and conducting mixed methods research (3rd ed.). SAGE.

Crosby, E., McKeage, K., Rittenburg, T. L., & Adkins, N. R. (2022). Amplifying marginalized consumers' voices: A case for trauma-informed qualitative methodologies. *International Journal of Market Research, 65*(2–3), 320–339.

Currier, J. M., McDermott, R. C., Sanders, P., Barkham, M., Owen, J., Saxon, D., & Richards, P. S. (2024). Practice-based evidence for spiritually integrated psychotherapies: Examining trajectories of psychological and spiritual distress. *Journal of Counseling Psychology, 71*(4), 291–303.

Daniel, T. (2019). Toxic theology as a contributing factor in complicated mourning. *Journal of Pastoral Care & Counseling, 73*(4), 196–204.

Demasure, K. (2022). The loss of the self—Spiritual abuse of adults in the context of the Catholic church. *Religions, 13*(6), 509.

Doyle, T. P. (2009). The spiritual trauma experienced by victims of sexual abuse by Catholic clergy. *Pastoral Psychology, 58*(3), 239–260.

Ellis, H. M., Hook, J. N., Freund, C., Kranendonk, J., Zuniga, S., Davis, D. E., & Van Tongeren, D. R. (2023). Religious/spiritual abuse and psychological and spiritual functioning. *Spirituality in Clinical Practice.*

Ellis, H. M., Hook, J. N., Zuniga, S., Hodge, A. S., Ford, K. M., Davis, D. E., & Van Tongeren, D. R. (2022). Religious/spiritual abuse and trauma: A systematic review of the empirical literature. *Spirituality in Clinical Practice, 9*(4), 213.

Enroth, R. M. (1993). Churches that abuse. Zondervan.

Enroth, R. M. (1994). Recovering from churches that abuse. Zondervan.

Fernández, S. (2022). Victims are not guilty! Spiritual abuse and ecclesiastical responsibility. *Religions, 13*, 427.

Fetters, M. D., Curry, L. A., & Creswell, J. W. (2013). Achieving integration in mixed methods designs—principles and practices. *Health services research, 48*(6pt2), 2134–2156.

Freckelton, I. (1998). "Cults," calamities and psychological consequences. *Psychiatry, Psychology, and the Law, 5*(1), 1–46.

Fricker, M. (2007). Epistemic injustice: Power and the ethics of knowing. OUP Oxford.

Galatzer-Levy, I. R., Huang, S. H., & Bonanno, G. A. (2018). Trajectories of resilience and dysfunction following potential trauma: A review and statistical evaluation. *Clinical psychology review*, *63*, 41–55.

Gillum, T. L., Sullivan, C. M., & Bybee, D. I. (2006). The Importance of Spirituality in the Lives of Domestic Violence Survivors. *Violence Against Women*, *12*(3), 240–250.

Giorgi, A. (2009). *The descriptive phenomenological method in psychology: A modified Husserlian approach.* Duquesne University Press.

Goertzen, G. L., & Yancey, G. (2025). Church-Related Institutional Betrayal and Institutional Courage in Domestic Violence: As Viewed Through a Qualitative Lens. *Religions, 16*(5), 638.

Gray, J. S., LaBore, K. B., & Carter, P. (2021). Protecting the sacred tree: Conceptualizing spiritual abuse against Native American elders. *Psychology of Religion and Spirituality, 13*(2), 204–211.

Greer, T. M. (2024). African-Centered Spirituality as a Buffer of Psychological Symptoms Related to Specific Forms of Racism for African Americans. *Journal of Black Psychology*, *50*(2), 165–193.

Halonen, U., Aaltonen, M., Van Aerschot, L., & Pirhonen, J. (2025). Participation of persons living with dementia in research: A means to address epistemic injustice. *Dementia, 24*(5), 850–865.

Harrell, S. P. (2000). A multidimensional conceptualization of racism-related stress: Implications for the well-being of people of color. *American Journal of Orthopsychiatry, 70*(1), 42–57.

Heath, M. A., & Cutrer-Párraga, E. A. (2020). Healing after traumatic events: Aligning interventions with cultural background and religious and spiritual beliefs. *Psychology in the Schools, 57*(5), 718–734.

Hodge, D. R., Zidan, T., & Husain, A. (2024). How to work with Muslim clients in a successful, culturally relevant manner: A national sample of American Muslims share their perspectives. *Social Work, 69*(1), 53–63.

Hollier, J., Clifton, S., & Smith-Merry, J. (2022). Mechanisms of religious trauma amongst queer people in Australia's evangelical churches. *Clinical Social Work Journal, 50*(3), 275–285.

Hürten, M., Leimgruber, U., McEwan, T., & McPhillips, K. (2025). The politics of vulnerability concerning sexual and spiritual abuse in the Catholic Church. *Religions, 16*(2), 137.

Istratii, R., & Ali, P. (2023). A scoping review on the role of religion in the experience of IPV and faith-based responses in community and counseling settings. *Journal of psychology and theology, 51*(2), 141-173.

Johnson, J., & VanVonderen, J. (1991*). The subtle power of spiritual abuse: Recognizing and escaping spiritual manipulation and false spiritual authority within the church.* Bethany House.

Karaman, N., & Christian, M. (2020). "My hijab is like my skin color": Muslim women students, racialization, and intersectionality. *Sociology of Race and Ethnicity, 6*(4), 517–532.

Kathawalla, U. K., & Syed, M. (2021). Discrimination, life stress, and mental health among Muslims: A preregistered systematic review and meta-analysis. *Collabra: Psychology, 7*(1), 28248.

Koch, D., & Edström, L. (2022). Development of the Spiritual Harm and Abuse Scale. *Journal for the Scientific Study of Religion, 61*(2), 476–506.

Knapp, P. J. (2021). Understanding Religious Abuse and Recovery: Discovering Essential Principles for Hope and Healing. Wipf & Stock Publishers.

Langberg, D. (2020). Redeeming Power: Understanding Authority and Abuse in the Church. Brazos Press.

Latif, J., Dockrat, S., & Rassool, G. H. (2024). Integrating Spiritual Interventions in Islamic Psychology: A Practical Guide. Routledge.

Lateef, H., & Umarji, O. (2022). Black American Muslims: A study of religious identity and mental health. *Mental Health, Religion & Culture, 25*(8), 802–816.

Lewis, J. R. (2011). The Branch Davidians: Through the Lens of Jonestown. Alternative Spirituality and Religion Review, 2(1), 55–88.

Lohmann, S., Cowlishaw, S., Ney, L., O'Donnell, M., & Felmingham, K. (2024). The trauma and mental health impacts of coercive control: A systematic review and meta-analysis. *Trauma, Violence, & Abuse, 25*(1), 630–647.

McGraw, D. M., Ebadi, M., Dalenberg, C., Wu, V., Nash, B., & Nunez, L. (2019). Consequences of abuse by religious authorities: A review. *Traumatology, 25*(4), 242–255.

McLaughlin, M. M., Ahmad, S. S., & Weisman de Mamani, A. (2022). A mixed-methods approach to psychological help-seeking in Muslims: Islamophobia, self-stigma, and therapeutic preferences. *Journal of Consulting and Clinical Psychology, 90*(7), 568.

McPhillips, K. (2018). "Soul Murder": Investigating Spiritual Trauma at the Royal Commission. *Journal of Australian Studies, 42*(2), 231–242.

Meyer, I. H. (2003). Prejudice, social stress, and mental health in lesbian, gay, and bisexual populations: Conceptual issues and research evidence. *Psychological Bulletin, 129*(5), 674–697.

Mohamed, B., & Diamant, J. (2019). Black Muslims account for a fifth of all US Muslims, and about half are converts to Islam. Pew Research Center.

Mulvihill, N., Aghtaie, N., Matolcsi, A., & Hester, M. (2022). UK victim-survivor experiences of intimate partner spiritual abuse and religious coercive control and implications for practice. *Criminology & Criminal Justice, 23*(5), 773–790.

Muscatell, K. A., Alvarez, G. M., Bonar, A. S., Cardenas, M. N., Galvan, M. J., Merritt, C. C., & Starks, M. D. (2022). Brain–body pathways linking racism and health. *American Psychologist, 77(9)*, 1049.

Neal-Stanley, A. M., Morgan, J. C., & Allen, D. J. (2024). The religio-spiritual capital of the Black Church: A conceptual model for combatting antiblackness in the early years. *Early Childhood Research Quarterly, 69*, S118–S128.

Nsour, R. (2022). My reflections on spiritual abuse. Journal of Islamic Faith and Practice, 4(1), 129–146

Nurein, S. A., & Iqbal, H. (2021). Identifying a space for young Black Muslim women in contemporary Britain. *Ethnicities, 2*1(3), 433–453.

Oakley, L. R., Kinmond, K., & Blundell, P. (2024). Responding well to spiritual abuse: Practice implications for counseling and psychotherapy. *British Journal of Guidance & Counseling, 52*(2), 189–206.

Oakley, L. R., Kinmond, K., & Humphreys, J. (2018). Spiritual abuse in Christian faith settings: Definition, policy and practice guidance. *Journal of Adult Protection, 20*(3/4), 144–154.

Oyewuwo, O. B., & Walton, Q. L. (2023). "We Can Only Go So Far": Employing Intersectionality in Research with Middle-Class Black Women and Black Muslim Women. *Affilia*, *38*(4), 656-672.

Ozcan, O., Hoelterhoff, M., & Wylie, E. (2021). Faith and spirituality as psychological coping mechanisms among female aid workers: A qualitative study. *Journal of International Humanitarian Action, 6*(1), 15.

Panchuk, M. (2020). Distorting Concepts, Obscured Experiences: Hermeneutical Injustice in Religious Trauma and Spiritual Violence. *Hypatia, 35*(4), 607–625.

Pargament, K. I., & Exline, J. J. (2020). Working with Spiritual Struggles in Psychotherapy: From Research to Practice. The Guilford Press.

Pargament, K. I., & Exline, J. J. (2021). Religious and spiritual struggles and mental health: Implications for clinical practice. In Spirituality and Mental Health Across Cultures (pp. 395–412).

Pargament, K. I., Exline, J. J., Cowden, R. G., & Wilt, J. A. (2025). Are spiritual struggles the cause or effect of psychological problems (or both)? Empirical findings and their implications for research and practice. *Spirituality in Clinical Practice.* Advance online publication.

Pargament, K. I., & Lomax, J. W. (2013). Understanding and addressing religion among people with mental illness. *World Psychiatry, 12(1)*, 26–32.

Perry, S. (2024). Religious/spiritual abuse, meaning-making, and posttraumatic growth. *Religions, 15(7)*, 824.

Pew Research Center. (2019). Black Muslims account for a fifth of all U.S. Muslims, and about half are converts to Islam. Pew Research Center Religion & Public Life Project.

Plaisime, M. V., Jipguep-Akhtar, M., Locascio, J. J., Belcher, H. M., Hardeman, R. R., Picho-Kiroga, K., ... & Dovidio, J. F. (2023). The impact of neighborhoods and friendships on interracial anxiety among medical students and residents: A report from the medical student CHANGES study. *Health services research, 58*, 229–237.

Platovnjak, I. (2024). Human vulnerability, spiritual abuse, and its prevention. *Obnovljeni Život, 79(2)*, 199-212.

Potz, M. (2019). Religious Legitimation of Power and the Concept of Theocracy. In Political Science of Religion: Theorizing the Political Role of Religion (pp. 63–85). Cham: Springer International Publishing.

Powell, R., & Pepper, M. (2021). *National Anglican family violence research report: Top line results.* NCLS Research Report. NCLS Research.

Ramler, M. E. (2023). When God hurts: The rhetoric of religious trauma as epistemic pain. *Rhetoric Society Quarterly, 53*(2), 202–216.

Ranjbar, N., Erb, M., Mohammad, O., & Moreno, F. A. (2020). Trauma-informed care and cultural humility in the mental health care of people from minoritized communities. *Focus, 18*(1), 8–15.

Rekis, J. (2023). Religious identity and epistemic injustice: An intersectional approach. *Hypatia, 38,* 779–800.

RHEE, T. Y. (2024). WHEN SHEPHERDS SCATTER GOD'S FLOCK: UNDERSTANDING SPIRITUAL ABUSE IN PREACHING. *Journal of the Evangelical Homiletics Society, 24*(1).

Rippy, A. E., & Newman, E. (2024). Discrimination, life stress, and mental health among Muslims: A meta-analytic review. *Collabra: Psychology, 7*(1), 28248.

Sanchini, V., Sala, R. & Gastmans, C. (2022). The concept of vulnerability in aged care: A systematic review of argument-based ethics literature. *BMC Med Ethics 2*3, 84.

Sharifnia, A. M., Bulut, H., Ali, P., & Rogers, M. (2023). Muslim women's experiences of domestic violence and abuse: A meta-ethnography of global evidence. *Trauma, Violence, & Abuse, 24*(4), 868–883.

Shengold, L. (1989). *Soul murder: The effects of childhood abuse and deprivation.* Yale University Press.

Shi, C., Ren, Z., Zhao, C., Zhang, T., & Chan, S. H. W. (2021). Shame, guilt, and posttraumatic stress symptoms: A three-level meta-analysis. *Journal of Anxiety Disorders, 82,* 102443.

Simonič, B., Mandelj, T. R., & Novšak, R. (2013). Religion-related abuse in the family. *Journal of Family Violence, 28*(4), 339–349.

Smith, P., & Freyd, J. J. (2014). Institutional Betrayal. *American Psychologist, 69*(6), 575–587.

Smidt, A. M., Adams-Clark, A. A., & Freyd, J. J. (2023). Institutional courage buffers against institutional betrayal, protects employee health, and fosters organizational commitment following workplace sexual harassment. *PLOS ONE, 18*(1), e0278830.

Stanton, C.E. (2020). Behavioral Health and Muslim Clients: Considerations for Achieving Positive Outcomes. In: Benuto, L.T., Gonzalez, F.R., Singer, J. (eds) Handbook of Cultural Factors in Behavioral Health. Springer, Cham.

Stone, S. N. (2024). Religious indoctrination: Psychological effects. In Encyclopedia of Religious Psychology and Behavior (pp. 1–6). Springer Nature.

Tineo, P., Bonumwezi, J. L., & Lowe, S. R. (2021). Discrimination and posttraumatic growth among Muslim American youth: Mediation via PTSD symptoms. *Journal of Trauma and Dissociation, 22*(2), 188–201.

Van der Kolk, B. (2014). The Body Keeps the Score: Brain, Mind, and Body in the Healing of Trauma. Viking.

Van Manen, M. (2023). *Phenomenology of practice: Meaning-giving methods in phenomenological research and writing*. Routledge.

Van Velzen, B. (2022). Weaponization of Faith. In World Christianity and COVID-19: Looking Back and Looking Forward (pp. 93–106). Springer International Publishing.

Vis, J.A., & Boynton, H. M. (2024). A spiritually integrated approach to trauma, grief, and loss: Applying a competence framework for helping professionals. *Religions, 15*(8), 931.

Walsh, F. (2020). Loss and resilience in the time of COVID-19: Meaning making, hope, and transcendence. *Family Process, 59*, 898–911.

Ward, D. J. (2011). The lived experience of spiritual abuse. Mental Health, *Religion & Culture, 14*(9), 899–915.

Weisman de Mamani, A., McLaughlin, M., Altamirano, O., Lopez, D., & Ahmad, S. S. (2021). Culturally informed therapy for schizophrenia: A family-focused cognitive behavioral approach: Clinician guide. Oxford University Press.

Williams, D. R., Lawrence, J. A., & Davis, B. A. (2019). Racism and health: Evidence and needed research. *Annual Review of Public Health, 40*, 105–125

Williams, M. T., Osman, M., Gallo, J., Pereira, D. P., Gran-Ruaz, S., Strauss, D., Lester, L., George, J. R., Edelman, J., & Litman, L. (2022). A clinical scale for the assessment of racial trauma. *Practice Innovations, 7*(3), 223–240.

Winell, M. (2011). Religious Trauma Syndrome. *Cognitive Behavioral Therapy Today, 39*(3), 16–18.

Appendix A:

Semi-Structured Interview Protocol

Purpose and Rationale

The semi-structured interview protocol is designed to examine the intersection of spiritual abuse, racial trauma (including intrareligious harm), and psychological distress among African American Muslims. Guided by trauma-informed interviewing principles, this protocol emphasizes participant agency, voice, and emotional safety, recognizing the historical marginalization of this population (Alessi & Kahn, 2022; Crosby et al., 2022).

The interviews, conducted by the principal investigator, will use open-ended questions organized into three overarching thematic areas: Spiritual Abuse, Racial Trauma (including intrareligious), and Psychological Distress. Questions are designed to facilitate in-depth narratives while remaining sensitive to potential emotional distress.

Trauma-Informed Safeguards

• Each interview will begin with rapport-building questions (e.g., "Can you tell me a little about your faith background?").

• Participants will be reminded that they may pause, skip questions, or end the interview at any time.

• The interviewer will monitor for signs of emotional distress, offer breaks, and provide grounding strategies as needed.

• A debriefing will be conducted at the end of each session, with referrals to mental health or community resources offered when appropriate.

* For Muslims, 'scripture' should be taken to mean either the Quran or the Hadiths (Oral and practiced traditions of the Prophet Muhammad).

Thematic Area 1: Spiritual Abuse

These questions explore experiences of spiritual harm, particularly focusing on three spiritual abuse mechanism domains: 1) Toxic Theological Interpretations, 2) Patriarchal (Male-Dominated) Leadership, and 3) Epistemic Injustice (i.e., the silencing or devaluing of individuals' voices, perspectives, and religious knowledge). The questions aim to uncover how participants perceive, interpret, and navigate these dynamics within religious spaces.

Core Open-Ended Questions:

- Have you ever experienced situations where religious teachings or interpretations felt hurtful, coercive, or used to control you?

- Can you describe a time when a religious leader or authority figure used their position of power in a way that felt spiritually or emotionally damaging?

- How have religious teachings or messages about obedience, sin, or morality affected you personally or spiritually?

- Have you ever felt silenced, dismissed, or invalidated when expressing your understanding of faith or scripture*?

- Have you had an incident or experience that you viewed as emotionally, mentally, or physically hurtful that was silenced, dismissed, or invalidated based on an alternative religious-based interpretation of faith or scripture*?

- Can you recall moments where religious teachings or practices conflicted with your personal well-being or spiritual autonomy?

- Can you describe an experience where religious teachings or interpretations felt harmful, coercive, or controlling?

- Have you experienced moments where religious authority figures misused their power in ways that caused harm?

- In what ways have gender or leadership structures influenced your spiritual experience?

- Have your religious insights or lived experiences ever been dismissed or devalued by leaders or community members?

- How did these experiences impact your trust in religious authority or your faith community?

Spiritual Abuse Follow-Up Questions via SA Mechanisms

Toxic Theological Interpretations:

- Were there specific interpretations of scripture* or doctrine that felt hurtful?

- Were there specific interpretations of scripture, religious laws, or moral teachings that you felt were weaponized or harmful?

- Were such interpretations used to justify harmful behaviors or silence questioning?

- How did these interpretations affect your relationship with God or your faith?

Patriarchal Leadership:

- How have male-dominated leadership structures shaped your experiences of voice, inclusion, or exclusion?

- Have you witnessed or experienced gender-based spiritual hurt?

- How have gendered power dynamics or male-dominated leadership structures influenced your experiences of voice, inclusion, or spiritual authority?
- Have you ever felt marginalized, controlled, or excluded due to these dynamics?

Epistemic Injustice:

- Have you felt silenced, ignored, or misrepresented in religious discussions or decision-making?
- How did these experiences affect your confidence in expressing your beliefs or engaging in religious spaces?
- Can you describe a time when your religious knowledge, spiritual experiences, or questions were dismissed or undervalued?
- How has this impacted your sense of belonging and authority within your faith community?
- How did these experiences affect your confidence in expressing your beliefs or engaging in religious spaces?

Thematic Area 2: Racial Trauma (Including Intrareligious Discrimination)

This section examines experiences of racial discrimination and cultural exclusion, both within broader society and in Muslim spaces. This section examines participants' experiences of racial discrimination, cultural exclusion, and intrareligious bias within both wider society and Muslim spaces. The questions aim to uncover how racial identity intersects with religious belonging, how these experiences are internalized, and the ways they influence spiritual well-being.

Core Open-Ended Questions:

- Have you experienced racial discrimination or bias in your faith community or Muslim spaces?

- Can you share a specific experience where your racial identity shaped how you were treated within a religious or community setting?

- Have you ever felt excluded, overlooked, or marginalized because of your race or cultural background?

- In what ways have racial stereotypes or assumptions impacted your interactions with religious leaders or peers?

- Have you experienced intrareligious discrimination—such as being treated as less authentic or less knowledgeable about your faith—because of your race or cultural heritage?

- How have these experiences affected your sense of belonging in your faith community?

- Have you experienced racial discrimination in your faith community or other Muslim spaces?

- How did these experiences affect your sense of belonging as an African American Muslim?

- Can you share a time when your racial identity influenced how religious leaders or community members treated you?

- Have you experienced spiritual hurt (pain/mistreatment) as a result of combined racism with religious authority or scripture* interpretation?

Additional Follow-Up Probes:

- Were there moments when religious teachings, practices, or community norms reinforced racial hierarchies or exclusion?

- How did these experiences make you feel emotionally and spiritually?

- Have these experiences changed how you view or engage with your faith or religious spaces?

- How have you responded or coped with moments of racial discrimination within the Muslim community?

- Have you found support or solidarity from others who share your racial or religious background?

- Are there specific events or turning points that stand out as particularly impactful in shaping your sense of identity?

- Were there patterns or incidents of exclusion that stood out as particularly significant?

- How did these experiences shape your understanding of race and faith?

- Did you ever feel that your identity as an African American Muslim was questioned or invalidated by other Muslims?

- How have you navigated intracommunal racism and its spiritual implications?

Thematic Area 3: Psychological Distress

This section addresses the emotional and mental health impacts of spiritual abuse and racial trauma while exploring coping strategies and sources of resilience. The questions aim to understand how these experiences have influenced participants' mental health, emotional regulation, and spiritual connection.

Core Open-Ended Questions:

- How have the experiences you've described affected your mental and emotional well-being?

- Have you experienced feelings of anxiety, depression, or spiritual disconnection as a result of these experiences?

- Can you describe any lasting emotional or psychological effects that stand out for you?

- How have these experiences influenced your sense of self-worth or identity?

- In what ways, if any, have these experiences affected your relationships with others (e.g., family, community, or religious leaders)?

- Have you noticed changes in your ability to trust others, participate in faith practices, or feel safe in spiritual spaces?

- Have you found it challenging to talk about these experiences with others or seek help?

Additional Follow-Up Probes:

- What emotions (such as anger, fear, or sadness) do you associate most strongly with these experiences?

- Have you noticed any changes in your sleep, energy, or daily functioning due to these experiences?

- How have you navigated or coped with these emotional impacts over time?

- Are there moments when you've felt healing, strength, or renewal despite the challenges?

- What practices or resources have supported your healing process?

- How do you maintain spiritual well-being despite these challenges?

Closing Questions

- How have you made sense of these experiences over time?
- Did these experiences change how you see your faith community or your spiritual journey?
- What steps, if any, have you taken to heal from these experiences or reclaim your spiritual voice?
- Is there anything we have not discussed that you feel is important to share?

Appendix B

The Spiritual Harm and Abuse Scale (SHAS)
(Koch & Edstrom, 2022)

Participant Instructions: This 27-item self-report instrument is designed to assess experiences of spiritual harm and abuse. Please read each statement carefully and indicate the extent to which each one reflects your personal experience within a spiritual or religious context.

Response Scale: Please give ONLY one Response for each question

1 – Strongly Disagree

2 – Disagree

3 – Neither Agree nor Disagree

4 – Agree

5 – Strongly Agree

There are no right or wrong answers. Please respond with honesty and reflect on your own experiences.

1   My behavior was excessively monitored by my spiritual leader or group.

2   My Imam or leader claimed to speak directly on God's behalf to control behavior.

3   I was expected to follow personal rules/advice from my Imam about dating, marriage, or sex.

4   Spiritual authority was used to direct choices in private life.

5   I feared the consequences of questioning my imam's authority.

6   Scripture or spiritual teachings were used to justify abusive parent-child behavior.

7   I was pressured to stay in an abusive marriage by religious leaders.

8   Leaving the community was portrayed as risking spiritual punishment (e.g., Hell).

9   The Quran and Sunnah texts were used to enforce submission or silence dissent.

10   Leadership protected or elevated individuals who had caused harm.

11   The system discouraged reporting or accountability for abuse.

12   Cultural or spiritual norms enforced loyalty above personal well-being.

13   Questioning institutional practices was discouraged or punished.

14   The institutional image was prioritized over individuals' safety and the truth.

15   Women (or certain genders) were explicitly or implicitly valued less in my spiritual context.

16   Gender roles were enforced in ways that caused me harm or restricted my freedom.

17   I was made to feel defective or spiritually flawed.

18   My doubts or questions about faith were dismissed as dangerous or faithless.

19   I felt spiritually unsafe within my community.

20   Religious expectations undermined my sense of self.

21   Shame was used to enforce spiritual conformity.

22   I experienced emotional or psychological distress tied to religious teachings.

23   Spiritual messaging caused lasting internal conflict or guilt.

24   Spiritual experiences were invalidated or made to feel untrustworthy.

25   I was taught that God would punish me harshly for questioning or disagreeing with those considered knowledgeable.

26   Suffering was framed as evidence of personal spiritual failure.

27   My relationship with the divine was portrayed as conditional or fear-based.

Appendix C

The Racial Trauma Scale

Instructions: Think about all the times when you have heard about, seen, or experienced racial discrimination. As a result of this, how bothered have you been by the following:

Response Scale: Please give ONLY one Response for each question

1   – Never

2   – Rarely

3   – Sometimes

4   – Often

5   – Always

1. Thinking the world is unsafe.

2. Feeling disconnected from myself.

3. Using alcohol to help me cope.

4. Feeling unsafe in public.

5. Having difficulties connecting with other people.

6. Using drugs to deal with my feelings.

7. Worrying about my loved one's safety.

8. Feeling nervous in social situations.

9. Using prescription medication to help with feelings.

10. Feeling society is unfair to people like me.

11. Fear that I will embarrass myself or others.

12. Causing myself physical pain (like cutting, burning, or hitting myself).

13. Thinking that others are purposefully working against me.

14. Feeling tired or as if I have less energy.

15. Sleeping too much.

16. Feeling watched by others.

17. Feeling worthless.

18. Weight changes without me trying.

19. Noticing people are less friendly to me.

20. Feeling like a failure.

21. Inability to stop moving.

22. Feeling on edge around people who might be racists.

23. Thinking I cannot reach my goals.

24. Reacting angrily.

25. Avoiding certain situations or speaking to certain people.

26. Feeling like I am not as good as others.

27. Thinking about ways to make other people suffer.

28. Watching my surroundings for danger.

29. Feeling like I cannot succeed.

30. Having nightmares about discrimination.

Add all items (1–30) for a total score on the RTS. Total scores range from 30 to 120. The three subscales are as follows: (a) Lack of Safety: 1, 4, 7, 10, 13, 16, 19, 22, 25, 28; (b) Negative Cognitions: 2, 5, 8, 11, 14, 17, 20, 23, 26, 29; (c) Difficulty Coping: 3, 6, 9, 12, 15, 18, 21, 24, 27, 30.

Appendix D

Integration Protocol — Narrative-Weaving of Quantitative and Qualitative Findings

Purpose

This protocol documents the step-by-step procedures for integrating the quantitative and qualitative strands of the study through narrative weaving. The integration approach privileged a dialogical stance in which quantitative patterns were contextualized by qualitative narratives and divergences were used to refine interpretation. The protocol ensures transparency, reproducibility, and an audit trail for all integration decisions.

Principles and Stance

- Dialogical integration: Treat quantitative and qualitative outputs as conversational partners; neither strand is presumed primary.

- Contextualization: Use narratives to explain, humanize, and give a mechanism to statistical patterns.

- Iterative refinement: Use points of divergence to prompt re-analysis, deeper coding, or targeted follow-back analyses.

- Transparency: Log all integration decisions, memos, and changes to interpretation.

Goals of Integration

1. Explain statistical associations through participant narratives.

2. Identify mechanisms that link exposures to outcomes.

3. Characterize areas of convergence, partial agreement, silence, and dissonance.

Construct Alignment

1. Map key quantitative constructs (e.g., spiritual abuse scale, distress outcome, race-based stressors) to qualitative codes and themes.

    - Linked qualitative codes/themes

2. Resolve mismatches: where no clear qualitative code maps to a quantitative construct, document as "qualitative silence" for follow-up.

3. Build joint displays to support narrative weaving

    - Case-linked display: individual qualitative case summaries alongside that case's quantitative scores (when permissible).

Narrative-weaving procedure (operational steps)

1. Identify focal quantitative findings to explain (e.g., strongest predictors, significant interactions, unexpected nulls). Prioritize by effect size and theoretical relevance.

2. For each focal finding, extract 2–4 salient qualitative excerpts that speak to that phenomenon.

3. Compose a concise integrative vignette: begin with the quantitative pattern, embed qualitative quotes to illustrate mechanisms, and end with an interpretive claim that links both strands.

4. Re-examine analytical choices in both strands.

Decision rules for claims

1. Strong integrated claim: convergence across strands (quantitative significance + clear qualitative mechanism).

2. Tentative integrated claim: quantitative or qualitative support exists, but with partial fit, unresolved silences. State uncertainty.

3. Divergent claim: persistent dissonance that illuminates complex or conditional processes; present as a substantive finding rather than error.

Documentation and audit trail

Maintain a record of the following: Quantitative SPSS Outputs, Qualitative Codebooks, Coding Summaries, and files, Personal Experience Themes (PETs) (participants' interview audio/visual recordings and written transcribed transcripts), and Group Experience Themes (GET), and dated entries.

Reporting conventions

- In write-up, present integrated findings as narrative vignettes built from joint displays; explicitly note integration code (e.g., convergence, elaboration, dissonance) for transparency.